WHAT'S BEEN SAID ABOUT GETTING UNSTUCK

"Most books about a sport give out information. They increase the sum of what we know. Tim O'Connor's new book provides the possibility of transformation; a shift in what we believe and how we view our world. *Getting Unstuck* offers wisdom that can reshape your entire golfing experience. Through his own authenticity, Tim shows that when you get through your blocks and blind spots, what emerges is an independent, resourceful, confident golfer. I see the book as a heartfelt intervention in what is almost a certain future for those of us who play the game."

Fred Shoemaker, Founder of Extraordinary Golf

"I firmly believe we are on the edge of a tipping point with golf. In a world of influencers and quick-fix promises, golfers are craving a deeper relationship to the game. In *Getting Unstuck*, Tim O'Connor provides you with a wonderfully rich and personal path to self-mastery. What you are about to read in these pages is an authentic journey of discovery which can help you peel back the layers and reveal what you are truly capable of. The wisdom contained in his book can be profoundly beneficial to your relationship with golf and to your life. Explore what is possible and allow Tim to be your guide. You are in very safe hands."

Karl Morris, Performance Coach, Founder of The Mind Factor

"Tim O'Connor's *Getting Unstuck* is for curious golfers who are ready to find a new perspective about this beautiful game. Sharing from his heart, Tim presents wisdom, humour and insights that will resonate with all golfers. The practices presented here have allowed me to play with strong inner peace. Even his footnotes are amazing!"

Susie Meyers, PGA of America,
Author of Golf from Point A

"If there's a golfer anywhere who hasn't been 'stuck,' I'd like to meet that person. Tim O'Connor has been there himself and has developed practical strategies to find freedom and clarity. Reading his book *Getting Unstuck* and applying its ideas will help you play better—really 'play'—and enjoy the game more."

Lorne Rubenstein, Author, Ontario and
Canadian Golf Halls of Fame Member

"I'm a golf nerd. I have a bumper sticker that says: 'Life is easy—golf is hard.' Until I picked up Tim O'Connor's book, I was *unconscious of what caused my golf-related suffering*. Getting Unstuck has helped me break free of that old way of being. Discovering a pathway to freedom in golf has helped me recover joy not only in golf, but in my life as well."

George Daranyi, Former Chairman of
The ManKind Project International

GETTING UNSTUCK

GETTING UNSTUCK

7 Transformational Practices for Golf Nerds

HOW TO CHANGE YOUR SELF-DEFEATING BEHAVIOURS AND MOVE YOUR GAME FORWARD

TIM O'CONNOR

For Sandy,
My love, my rock

CONTENTS

FOREWORD

By "Humble" Howard Glassman

I knew Tim before I met him from reading his book, *The Feeling of Greatness: The Moe Norman Story.*

I loved his biography of the enigmatic golf genius whose ball-striking was legendary. But the book also showcased something about the author that I would later come to understand as Tim's superpower: his empathy.

I met Tim years later when he interviewed a much less-accomplished golfer—me—for a profile for a magazine published for members of golf clubs owned by Canadian company Club-Link. During our initial chat, Tim and I spent a lot of time geeking out about golf swings, golfers, and courses, but mostly we talked about what the game meant to us and how frustrated we had been at various times in our golf lives.

The first book I ever read on the mental side of the sport was *Golf is Not a Game of Perfect* by renowned sport psychologist Bob Rotella. That book was like a gateway drug for me and opened the door to many others of that ilk that helped me transition from a sulky, pouty, suck of a player who was one bad swing away from melting down and possibly quitting in the middle of the round, to a much less sulky, pouty, suck who could keep his "big boy" pants on for most of the round.

To my delight, I found I had this in common with Tim. To be fair, I knew Tim had not broken as many clubs as I had, but he could certainly relate and, more importantly, empathize. That's what he does best: he listens and relates. From those early meetings, a quick friendship was born based on our mutual fascination with why we and other golfers couldn't figure out a better way to navigate our mental minefields.

His published article captured my obsession with the game but didn't make me out to be a golf lunatic. We enjoyed our conversations so much that we wanted to keep them going; so, we started a podcast. This was nine years ago when many of you thought a podcast was something that your coffee pods did.

Given that our focus was the mental and strategic side of golf, we called it *Swing Thoughts*! We hoped people would dig the clever irony because we almost never talk about actual golf swings; instead, we focus on finding ways to help golfers, ourselves included, to enjoy the game more and to play better.

We've recorded over 250 episodes together featuring wide-ranging discussions with some of the biggest names in the mental game, including Karl Morris, Ellen Langer, Gabriele Wulf, Dr. Raymond Prior, Paul Dewland, Ed Coughlan, Mike Hebron, and Fred Shoemaker. We've also interviewed swing gurus such as Sean Foley, Martin Chuck, and legend David Leadbetter.

Through it all, I've had the privilege of seeing Tim grow as a broadcaster and enjoyed learning ideas and concepts that have helped our audience to understand themselves and this game a bit better. I know that Tim and I have benefited as well.

I've witnessed Tim's growing knowledge of the game as a coach, player, and student of the game. We understand a lot of the same things, but he comes at them from a different perspective that is informed by his aforementioned superpower!

He gets that from years of being involved in the ManKind Project, which helps men unlock their inner assholes and get in better touch with the real person that lives inside.

This gives Coach Tim, as I call him, a unique ability to understand how the human condition—especially where male golfers are concerned—affects us as golfers, and how our thinking and emotions can make golf a miserable experience for us and the people we interact with.

Tim also brings a humanity to his instruction because he's not afraid to show who he is. He doesn't come off as a guru with all the answers, but more like a seasoned traveler who can give some guidance because he's visited the places you've been and he can help you avoid the sketchier parts of town!

One of my favourite Tim stories is about first time we played. We had been yammering for a couple of months about the mental game and how it had impacted our game and life when we finally teed it up together at Glencairn, my club just west of Toronto.

Well, I watched this dude, who I really didn't know too well, shank every iron shot from No. 4 to 16. Every iron shot! Pretty awkward stuff especially for your first game with a relative stranger. Many people would have been embarrassed. Or they'd get angry or be pissy to play with.

Tim was none of that. He acknowledged the shanks, of course. And they were a drag for sure, but he wasn't. I remember thinking how impressive he was that day. I came away knowing that this was a solid dude who had done the work and understood what was important about this ridiculous game.

Nine years later, I continue to be impressed.

He has absorbed a vast amount of golf wisdom along with some important life lessons and experience, and he's more than qualified to pass that on to anyone lucky enough to have a coaching session with him.

He's now passing on what he's learned to you by applying his award-winning skill as a writer.

In *Getting Unstuck: Seven Transformational Practices for Golf Nerds*, you'll get some practical lessons that will definitely grow your game. The book is not about changing your swing, but more importantly, it's a road map to a different way of experiencing yourself and the game.

It will provide you with a way out of "golf hell" if that's your predicament, and a pathway to thinking differently about your game that might end up lowering your scores.

I can promise you that *Getting Unstuck* will lead to another type of golf—one that you'll enjoy more on a deeper level than you ever have before.

"Humble" Howard Glassman
Co-host of the legendary *Humble & Fred*
radio program and podcast; Co-host of the
Swing Thoughts podcast with Tim O'Connor

INTRODUCTION

**"I was looking for love in
all the wrong places."**

Johnny Lee

The pursuit of becoming a "good golfer" is a seductive trap that feasts upon your desires, compulsions, beliefs, and the stories you tell about yourself. How do I know? I lived it.

Like you, I've raged, slammed, tossed, and done unspeakable violence to golf clubs, moped and sulked, questioned and pleaded, hit balls until my hands blistered, worked my way through 27 swing thoughts in nine holes, and run to the range in panic.

I've sought salvation in better hip turn, more vigorous hand action, taken lessons, damaged drywall with a training device, gone to golf schools, read the books, bought more training devices, watched the videos, torn pages from *Golf Digest*, and been forbidden from bringing training devices near glassware.

And yet, for most of my golf life, I remained mired in mediocrity, stuck on a plateau where I glimpsed islets of light and savoured shots that felt so easy that I believed I had finally solved golf—only to realize it was a puff of smoke.

Sound familiar? Of course it does.

As a fellow golf nerd, I know that you don't just want to get better at golf—you crave it.[1]

Otherwise, you wouldn't invest so much of your time, money, and sense of yourself in your zeal to become more "consistent," lower your index, and fix your nemesis shots. And—if you're honest—try to look good to others and become known as a "good golfer."

Or seek books like this.

In your desire to *improve* and become *better*, like pretty well every golf nerd I ever met, you've been chasing, pursuing, and questing ever so nobly for the code that will unlock the vault of the golf gods in the belief that their sacred secrets will elevate you to the hallowed "next level" that you so justly deserve.

The golf culture feeds on your craving by promising that if you improve, you will reach the zenith of our culture: you will be happy. If this sounds like a morality tale of goodness versus evil, of being saintly versus giving into temptation, of following a path of virtue versus gratification, that's not the intent.

What I'm offering you is a practical guide to finally making the transformation that you've been seeking so you can get

---

[1] I've borrowed "golf nerd" from my *Swing Thoughts* podcast partner Howard Glassman to describe people like you and I. Golf nerd is much more viscerally appropriate and descriptive than "avid," not as over-the-top as "obsessive," nor as demeaning as "geek," which seems more fitting for that wretched kid in Grade 7 who got 100 per cent on math tests and smelled like vegetable soup but is now a tech millionaire.)

unstuck, stop flitting from tip to tip, and cycling through bouts of hope and despair only to find yourself disappointed yet again.

This book directs your attention to places where you've likely never looked before—at the thoughts, feelings and behaviours that have shackled you, and how to release yourself from the hold they have upon you.

I'm also offering you the benefit of some well-earned experience and research that is counter-intuitive to the culture of golf: namely, your inability to "get better" isn't that you can't convince your various body parts to work together to hit soft draws and butter cuts on demand.

What keeps you stuck is not your lack of athleticism, that you haven't found the right information, that you started late, that you have too many bad habits, that you are a choking dog, or that your dad yelled at you. You are stuck not because you can't keep your head down, transfer your weight, or swing on plane.

You are stuck because of the way you habitually think, feel, and behave. You are stuck because of patterns that prevent you from staying committed to specific actions or, say, a mission that would allow you to develop solid skills.

You are stuck because of the thoughts and feelings that you give into, your reactions, and the decisions you make about the things that you believe you must do. Or more, accurately, you feel *compelled* to do.

You are stuck because of behaviours that relieve your anxiety and cravings and quell your undesirable feelings. At least temporarily.

If this sounds like we're in the territory of addiction, we're close.

You have arrived at your station in life based on beliefs about yourself, perceptions of the world, and unconscious strategies that kept you safe and allowed you to get a lot of what you wanted. You have deeply honed patterns of thinking and feeling that have created habitual patterns of behaviour that determine what you do. You have followed these patterns since you were a kid. They propelled you forward to the life you have.

But eventually—as everyone discovers—at a certain point, many of these patterns stop working. Their cost starts to outweigh the benefits. And the costs show up starkly in golf, in which we literally keep numerical score of everything we do.

You are stuck because you are looking for love in many of the wrong places.

How do I know this? I'm just like you.

And I'm not like you.

I don't mean that I'm superior in any way; I've just had experiences that most golf nerds don't have.

As a journalist and broadcaster, I've been fortunate to interview some pretty interesting people, including artists such as David Bowie, Peter Gabriel, the members of Pink Floyd and U2, Bryan Adams, and Joe Strummer; golfers such as Moe Norman, Tiger Woods, Jack Nicklaus, and Fred Couples; coaches such as Sean Foley, David Leadbetter, Bob Rotella, Karl Morris, and Fred Shoemaker; and academics such as Gabriele Wulf, Ellen Langer and Judson Brewer.

I have reported on U.S. Opens, PGA Championships, Masters, and Canadian Opens, both men's and women's. I covered the 1997 Masters when Tiger won his first major. I've facilitated men in emotional healing and shadow work for more than 20 years. I've taken singing lessons and improv comedy courses and become a professional public speaker. I play bass in a punk band.

In just about everything I've ever done, I wondered, "Could this help make me a better golfer?" It seems kind of ridiculous and even sick, but I'm a golf nerd. We're weird that way.

I believe that there's something far deeper at work for golf nerds than just wanting to play better, lower your handicap, win anything from C Flight to a major championship. I'm fascinated by the mystery of what propels us ever forward to seek mastery, but also what holds us back.

I've been driven to explore why, despite our collective efforts, the overwhelming majority of golf nerds feel stuck, incompetent, and even kind of stupid. My work has focused on the behaviours that keep us stuck, doing the same self-sabotaging things over and over again.

How do we break out of these behaviours, transform, and find joy, satisfaction and achieve genuine mastery?

That's what this book is about. Providing you not just with information that might be new and helpful to you, but seven practices that allow you to work through your challenges, transform your self-defeating behaviours, and develop pathways that lead to genuine improvement.

I've learned a lot from studying great artists, players and coaches, researching the work of experts in the fields of psychology, performance, and mindfulness, but I believe my most important lessons came from my lived experiences.

I've included several of my experiences in what I call "interludes" in this book. I believe that stories are powerful. When we read or listen to someone else's story, we relate to our own experience and often gain greater insights.

WHAT IF YOU'RE NOT A GOLF NERD?

Through the years, many people have told me that the stuff that I write and talk about is not just applicable to golf, but also to other parts of life.

Although you may not be a golf nerd, you are likely passionate—kind of crazy actually—about something that both fascinates and tortures you; you have a deep desire to "get better" or achieve a goal, but you often feel frustrated that you aren't making better progress. You feel stuck.

The practices in this book are foundational for elite performers in any field. By integrating practices that enhance and increase our self-awareness, we "sharpen the saw" as Stephen Covey says, and live more consciously, creatively and see what's truly possible for us.

With this book, I suggest you take a similar approach to golfers to whom I have recommended Timothy Gallwey's classic book *The Inner Game of Tennis*. I suggest they just replace the word tennis with the word golf.

You could do the same with this book by replacing golf with whatever you wish: playing guitar, investing, managing, parenting—or tennis.

A gift of grace

On the 18th green, I took off my hat, faked a smile, muttered "Good game" through gritted teeth, and shook hands with my partner. I pretended to be a good sport.

After signing my scorecard, I threw my pencil into the dashboard of my cart, floored the accelerator, and roared through the parking lot. I was in full-on angry mode. Livid.

My mind was going faster than the cart. "Oh my God, you fucking jerk! What kind of coach does that?" I slapped the steering wheel. "You're a coach! All the guys watched! The fucking golf coach. The mental game guy!"

Indeed, about 25 guys at the top of the hill overlooking the green had witnessed the four-putt that concluded the second round of my 2023 club championship at Blue Springs Golf Club, just west of Toronto. They watched my first putt from about 50 feet come up 10-woeful-feet short. The next putt slid by about 18 inches. Annoyed, I rushed it.

"Fuck!"

I tapped my fourth putt in for a triple-bogey seven.

At my car, I was spiraling into the vortex of a raging tantrum.

I whipped my golf shoes into the hatchback and took my bag off the cart and banged it noisily on the pavement. It was a signal to anyone in earshot to "stay the fuck away."

Just then, I heard: "Hey Tim, how was your day?"

I turned around. "Oh my God." It was Tim Casarin, smiling and standing behind his car. In that instant, I was caught. Exposed. Ridiculous.

We had just been reintroduced a few weeks earlier.

About a dozen years before, we were fellow hockey and soccer dads in our old neighbourhood. But as happens, our time chatting rink-side or waving hello when walking the dog was a distant memory. We had both moved, and Tim had become a full-time fire fighter.

In 2014, Tim and his firehall mates answered a call to a warehouse in Mississauga; smoke was pouring out of the roof but there were no flames. Unbeknownst to them, the warehouse was full of propane tanks, butane lighters and aerosol cans.

As they stood a few feet from the building, the warehouse exploded. A cinder-block wall fell on Tim and two colleagues, burying them under a pile of broken 50-pound blocks. Their comrades raced over and worked frantically to free them.

Two of the firefighters were severely injured but conscious. One was screaming. When they found Tim underneath the shards, his face mask was sideways, full of blood. His eyes fluttered open and closed. Thankfully, he was breathing—barely.

Two fire fighters each grabbed Tim underneath an arm and dragged him away from the inferno toward an ambulance.

Tim was in a medically induced coma for eight days. He suffered 41 broken bones, including a shattered face, fractured skull, shoulders, and pelvis. Days after the explosion, doctors learned that Tim's neck was also broken. He was later told that he'd likely walk with a cane for the rest of his life, and that the days of playing hockey and golf were over. He underwent 27 surgeries.

Within a year, amazingly, he was back at work. His firefighting buddies called him the "miracle man." He eventually made his way back to the gym, living a more "normal" life and, obviously, playing golf. His remarkable story of grit and resilience was rightly celebrated and told eagerly.

When Tim said hello in the parking lot, I froze. I was caught. A bad little boy having a hissy fit. A spoiled brat. A rush of blood made my cheeks feel like they were on fire. I thought: "Holy shit. You're facing a man who survived hell."

Words started to tumble awkwardly out of my mouth. I launched into my act—I faked that I was cool, chill, good. Gradually, the words picked up speed as I launched into my post-round lamentations. As I talked, my tragic bits became comic bits. I felt lighter with every word.

When I stopped babbling, Tim shared the ups and downs of his round. We laughed and commiserated about our foozles and foibles, as golfers do. We ended our chat with one of those promises that golfers make to get a game in.

In the days that followed the club championship—I finished well back, thank you—I thought about the incredible timing of Tim and I running into each other in the parking lot. Somehow the universe, God, or dumb luck—whatever works for you—made sure that at the moment I was suffering one of my meltdowns Tim and I should meet.

Tim reminded me that I can fall back into my old ways, but they don't define me like they once did; I can—eventually—work my way out of most of them.

There are very practical things that I can do—that anyone can do—to move forward as a golfer and as a person.

WHAT THIS BOOK
CAN DO FOR YOU

This book provides golf nerds with research, insights, anecdotes, and practices that allow you to get unstuck and transform your game and, quite possibly, your life. As a fellow golf nerd, I invite you to dive in, learn more about these practices, and to use them.

Crave is almost too weak a word to describe what you, a golf nerd, want from this game. If you're honest, you come pretty close to groveling before the golf gods.

As a golf nerd, you are forever searching and striving in your noble quest. Despite your heroic efforts, however, you always seem to be in a perpetual stall. You have not made the progress that you crave, and you wonder why.

This book is about getting you unstuck and moving forward. Moving from your old ways that are tied to the past to a new future as a golfer.

This book provides you with seven key practices that will allow you to make the progress you are seeking if you apply them on a regular and dedicated basis. They are simple and easy to do at home or anywhere. They don't require much time, or special equipment, incense, fasting, or going on a retreat or to bootcamp. These practices, all of which are rooted in tradition, neuroscience, and social science, are practical; they are not particularly trendy or the stuff of internet influencers.

If you engage in these practices, they will lead you to greater awareness, self-understanding and to taking action that transforms your golf. Most of these practices are rituals for elite performers in every realm of sport, the arts, and business.

None of these practices involves swinging a golf club, which you may surmise means that this book is about the mental game. Consider that everything that we do starts in the brain. Every decision you make about what you're going to improve, fix, eradicate, focus on, explore, and try to master begins in your mind.

I believe there are five facets of golf: technical, physical, mental, emotional, and spiritual. All five must be in balance to play the golf you're seeking. If you're focusing only on the technical and physical aspects of golf, you're subject to what's in your blind spots. Interestingly, by also tuning into what you're thinking, feeling, and exploring, you *will* develop far more awareness of the technical and physical aspects of your game.

This book outlines seven key practices that elite golfers and performers dedicate themselves to—to increase their self-awareness, make good on their commitments, stay on course, avoid distractions, learn more about themselves, gain perspective, develop mastery, and live and play in a way that makes their lives fulfilling and joyful.

COMMITTING TO FREEDOM

Tim Casarin and I played our game. In fact, we played a bunch, and we began to forge a deep connection. He told me about his amazing recovery and about talking to victims of catastrophic injuries and their caregivers, providing them with hope and inspiration, although he always deflects any notion that he's some kind of hero.

Tim fascinated me. I wondered what inspires a man who suffered 41 broken bones and 27 surgeries to not only learn how to walk again, but to live a robust life that includes being a vital part of his partner's and kids' lives, going to the gym, becoming a club fitter, and playing golf.

My emerging friendship with Tim reinforced the importance and value of honestly examining our lives, increasing our awareness of how we behave, and committing to actions that are aligned with a mission.

To me, people who have achieved mastery of any kind live in a way that is unwavering. They are committed to taking actions that lead them to the life they have chosen.

They have made a commitment to freedom. That seems completely contradictory. But I interpret "commit to freedom" as: my commitment frees me from rationalizing, making excuses, seeking reassurance, craving a desired result, giving in to my compulsions and addictions, and generally drifting through my life and allowing circumstances to dictate what I think, feel, and do.

When I stay true to my commitments, I am free of my self-pitying, raging, wailing ego nonsense that keeps me shackled to the past. The stuff that keeps me stuck.

It all sounds very noble, worthy of a monster rock anthem soundtrack featuring a Carlos Santana heroic guitar solo. It *is* all that, but making such a commitment doesn't come with reading a book, listening to podcasts, or absorbing inspirational tidbits as you scroll through your phone.

You can change your behaviours and actions a little based on information you've taken in. But you don't *transform* to a new way of being. Change is subject to change, especially backwards. Transformation is a portal to a new way of being. To getting unstuck.

Transformation usually comes from lessons learned from hard experiences—such as mistakes, accidents, a diagnosis, separation, and crises—the kind you hate when they happen but thank later for the perspective they provide. But transformation is also possible through commitment, integration, and a process of honest self-reflection and growing awareness.

PRACTICE / PROCESS / INTEGRATION / MASTERY

Like you—as a flawed human and golf nerd—I'm prone to being distracted, to seeking excitement and immediate gratification, and being sucked into my old behaviours. But through my experiences as a golf nerd, writer, and coach, I've learned and followed several practices that allowed me to get unstuck.

As Fred Shoemaker has said, "I'm not just a guy in a bar talking." This experience has allowed me to coach many of my clients to overcome their self-sabotaging beliefs, stories, and habits.

As a coach, I've learned that as golf nerds, we're all prone to the similar pitfalls:

- Through our addiction to results and our behaviours, we unconsciously grasp unto "fixes," advice, and expert models of the "right way."
- We flit from tip to tip, seeking the secret that will relieve our anxiety and feelings of inadequacy and incompetence.
- Unconscious to our habitual ways of thinking, feeling, and behaving, we lurch through much of our lives as if in a trance.
- We rarely stay with any discovery, insight or feeling long enough to fully explore, learn, and integrate it.
- We believe our salvation is in technical and mental tactics—things external to us—rather than learning from our own physical and inner experience.
- We don't follow a plan or mission; we aren't committed to a chosen path.
- We act according to our beliefs and stories about ourselves and the world.
- Our actions are dictated by our past, rather than by a future that we create and live into.

You likely relate to some these tendencies. They are among the key reasons that—despite your investment in time, money, blood, sweat and maybe even tears—you haven't made the progress that you've sought.

WHY I WROTE THIS BOOK

I believe that I can be service to more golf nerds by compiling a number of basic practices that—if you get past your resistance and actually do them—will allow you to better access your talent, skill, and experience as a golfer, and to live more consciously and intentionally in the rest of your life.

It's also my hope that this book answers some of these common questions and concerns of golf nerds:

- What are the essential practices that elite performers commit themselves to?
- How do I quiet my mind, stop being highjacked by my thoughts and emotions, and constantly questioning and criticizing myself?
- How do I get out of cycles of compulsively searching for tactics and devices that rarely deliver the results I'm seeking?
- How do I learn from my experiences with a sense of curiosity and detachment rather than suffering fits of drama, disappointment, and self-flagellation?
- How do I develop my game while recapturing the joy that first made me into a golf nerd?
- How can I learn how to play the golf I desire without moving into Sean Foley's basement, getting fired, becoming estranged from my family, and a miserable, ridiculous crank?
- How do I stop myself from repeatedly doing things I don't want to do, and do more of the things that I want to do?
- What is the foundation for making commitments, staying true to them, and taking action based on my commitments?

- What is the secret to avoiding distraction by the shiny new thing?

Through the seven practices in this book, you will draw on the richness of your own experiences and find that the secrets that you've been seeking have been within you all along.

As a golf nerd, you've heard how rotation creates centrifugal force that draws power outward causing the club to move quickly and powerfully. Golf culture is also like centrifugal force. Golf culture feeds upon your craving for results, happiness, and control, drawing you away from your centre into regions of desire, distraction, and unreality.

The practices in this book provide you with an opportunity to create a strong internal force and choose a path that allows you to learn from your own experiences and access the gold of your true self that's been there all the time.[1]

There are mountains of research, examples from elite players, and experiences to show that integrating these practices into your life will allow you to get unstuck and make the progress you've been seeking.

This book shows you the right place to look. Inside yourself.

---

[1] The Unquiet Monk: Thomas Merton's Questing Faith. Michael W. Higgins. Novalis.

The irony of finding freedom in a commitment

In the days following my 2023 club championship, I thought that as a coach I didn't walk my talk. Rather than stay committed to my process, I defaulted to my old ways—addicted to outcomes and falling back on old swing thoughts.

And getting mad like that? Really? One of my favourite sayings is the adage that comes with the inferred moral: "You're not good enough to get mad."

As a coach, I preach commitment and accountability, but as a golf nerd I can be as distracted, seduced, and ultimately dissatisfied as most people that I coach. That is, I become like a flimsy rowboat tossed around on the seas of my self-generated torment, searching for a beacon that I believe will bring me the result that I'm seeking. As the saying goes, any port in a storm will do.

In my arrogance, I had not sought coaching for a few years. But encountering Tim Casarin was a gift not to be wasted. I sent an email to legendary coach Fred Shoemaker, with whom I'm fortunate to have a relationship, and we arranged a coaching call.

I told Fred that I dedicated myself to playing golf in 2023 as if it were a purely physical game. I would do this by paying attention to the feeling of the club in my hands on every shot.

During my call with Fred, I admitted I had fallen back on my old patterns in the Club C, which resulted in having different swing thoughts for every part of my game. As always, Fred was direct, saying, "You were angry that you have to focus. You think you have trained yourself, but you haven't."

Ouch. Fred cut me to the core. I had not held myself accountable. I didn't stay *true* to my commitment.

Fred continued: "You need to train yourself so that you're saying: 'This shall be. I won't hit another ball until I stay with my commitment—to be present to my hands. Nothing will distract me.'

"But you've found ways to be distracted. You think that with knowledge and limited practice, you should be able to maintain your focus. This is not true. You have to train your capacity to be present and disregard any thoughts."

As Fred talked, I thought about the process of integration— committing to taking action with high frequency. Doing things until I owned them. Integration leads to skill development, self-reflection, accountability, observation, staying on a chosen path, and developing greater awareness of oneself.

Then Fred laid this nugget on me: "The only freedom that I found in golf was through a structure, and the only freedom I've found was through a commitment."

As a friend likes to say: Boom!

Don't Be Scared, It Ain't Weird— to Meditate

Things I love about golf:

- The feeling of a dead-solid-perfect iron shot.
- Watching a putt track to the hole that felt *in* from the get-go.
- A perfectly timed needling remark that is expressed as a ball heads towards oblivion.
- Posting a low score.
- A post-round celebratory libation with my group.
- How golf reveals myself more clearly to me.

Of all the things that golf offers—including the inherent challenge of hitting a small ball with a small implement, exercise in a beautiful space, and camaraderie—I also love how it acts as a mirror. Golf reveals our behaviours and patterns starkly and un-retouched. That's if we pay attention. If not, we miss the opportunity that golf presents to move toward what we're seeking in this game, and possibly in our lives. And you thought it was just about beating your obnoxious brother-in-law.

As a fellow golf nerd, I invite you not to miss that opportunity because it's where you will discover what's been holding you back in your zeal to reach your golf goals, and it can also reveal what you are truly capable of.

That discovery starts with paying attention; by observing your mind.

That may seem obtuse, but most of the time, we go through rounds of golf without a clue what our minds are doing. It's like we're in a trance, carried unconsciously this way and that by our thoughts, feelings, behaviours, and beliefs. That is no way to play golf or live your life.

The mistake that many golfers make is a belief that their thinking is their problem. Rather, it's their relationship with their thinking. Everyone has unhelpful thoughts; in fact, we all have thoughts that we'd never share lest our friends and family decide we're a menace to society.

Here's what I'm proposing: rather than unwittingly being caught up in your thinking, feelings, and behaviours—as, if you're honest, you normally do—I invite you to witness your mind as you play, practice, and in all parts of your life. Not control, manage, or change what your mind does. Just witness.

To transform your relationship with your mind, you must first become aware of its tendencies, content, behaviours, and more. Transformation is impossible without awareness of what's in your blind spots.

To make the breakthroughs that you're seeking in your game, you must be aware of what your mind is doing. Otherwise, you'll keep doing what you've always done, which for most golfers includes chasing tips and techniques, getting caught up in drama, forever being distracted, and seeking solutions to make their fantasies come true. (Fantasies of soft draws and laser-guided approaches, that is.)

How do you witness your mind?

I suggest that you start by viewing it as an entity that's separate from you. That's radical for most people. Mostly, we live our lives according to our thoughts and beliefs. We tend to go through life as if every thought *is* just the way life is.

Our brains default to a form of day-dreaming that keeps us chronically self-absorbed and re-thinking the same things day after day. Estimates of the number of thoughts we have a day range from 6,000 to 70,000. Regardless what is right, that's a lot of thoughts. And we tend to think the same thoughts day after day.

But it doesn't need to be that way. Your thoughts are not reality. They are just thoughts. Most people don't notice how identified they are with their thoughts. Your life changes when you become aware that you *have* thoughts, rather than your thoughts *have* you.

Here's a question for you:

Do you have *a mind? Or are* you *your mind?*

Consider the ramifications of your answer. One provides you with choice and freedom. The other makes you a victim of your mind, such as the person who rationalizes his or her behaviour—and often the quality of their golf—with "That's just who I am."

Being a victim means you give up your power. You're stuck, shackled to your past, your beliefs, shadows, stories, and behaviour patterns. No way out. Being a victim is a dead end.

When I say, "I am angry," or "I suck," I've identified myself with those feelings. "This is who I am." From this place, it's almost impossible to become emotionally neutral and make choices that serve you.

This next bit may sound strange, but changing anything requires getting uncomfortable and working through your resistance. Instead of getting caught up in your thoughts and feelings, you might find it helpful to say, "My mind is afraid that I'm going to screw up this round." Or "My mind is angry that I have three-putted twice." This is only possible if you view your mind as an entity separate from yourself.

Observing your mind provides you with opportunity, possibility, more freedom, and greater perspective. When you observe your mind, you can take advantage of a wonderful phenomenon:

Awareness is curative.

Just being aware of your mind decreases the intensity of your feelings, frees you from your usual thinking patterns, and from defaulting to behaviours that sabotage you.

This, of course, is not the way the majority of people relate to their feelings and thoughts. Historically, we have not been taught in Western culture to relate objectively to our minds, and to develop a relationship with our minds that allows us to make choices about what we're thinking, feeling, believing, and how they affect our behaviour.

That's why it's integral that you train your mind in the skill of awareness. If you just read this book, you will learn some things, but you won't change your relationship with your mind. Regardless of insights you may have, you will fall back into your old ways. Our brains resist change. Making a difference means doing new things *a lot*.

To develop your skill of awareness, you must commit to practices that allow you to integrate these new ways of being into your golf and life. In the same way that you won't develop your muscles by reading a book about weightlifting, you won't develop a healthier relationship with your mind unless you train it.

DEVELOPING THE SKILL OF AWARENESS

The No. 1 way to improve your relationship with your mind is to practice meditation.

If your first reaction is, "Yeah, right, meditation is woo woo," I get it. Or it reeks of McMindfulness like the self-help section in a bookstore. Perhaps you gave it a shot during a vacation with a bunch of folks in yoga pants, but figured it wasn't for you.

As Dan Harris wrote in *Ten Percent Happier*, meditation has a PR problem.[1] To paraphrase Harris, many golfers associate mediation with something mystical like levitating through some kind of cosmic goo to have tea with Buddha. Or you must

---

[1] If you are dubious about meditation, I suggest you read *Ten Percent Happier*. Harris, who describes himself as a "fidgety skeptic," debunks myths about meditation and provides a practical introduction to the practice. The podcast is also excellent.

renounce worldly things, light incense, and listen to sitar music.

Consider, however, that elite performers of all types meditate, including Michael Jordan, LeBron James, Carlie Lloyd, Aaron Rogers, Tom Brady, Serena Williams, Luke Donald, Rory McIlroy, and Wyndham Clark, as well as performing artists, and high-level business executives.

We've all watched athletes sitting alone on TV before a game with their eyes closed. They're meditating. Paul Dewland, mental coach to top tour players around the world, insists that all his clients have or begin a meditation practice.[2]

Here's a rough definition: meditation is the practice of noticing without judgment, struggle or effort to change or control anything. I have been meditating for about 20 years. I'm with Harris that it's made me a little less volatile and even lightened me up over the years, but I still screw up and get occasionally messed up. But I believe that meditation has increased my awareness so that I can respond more quickly and skillfully to my mind's shenanigans.

To me, being aware is one of the most practical and important things I can do in my golf and my life. Awareness is essential to executing any task and for effectively dealing with any situation, whether it's recovering from a drive out of bounds, driving a car safely, or negotiating a business deal. If you are distracted, caught up in thought and awash in negative emotions, you cannot perform near the peak of your talent, skills, and experiences.

---

[2]There are numerous studies citing how mindfulness practices such as meditation have improved the performance of athletes as well as their mental health.

Being unaware is no excuse for anything.[3]

I'll provide some direction on the very practical practice of meditation shortly, but first I'm going to address many of the misconceptions about meditation that I believe make some golfers resistant to it.

Many people have told me that they gave up on meditation because they weren't good at it—that they were "bad" meditators. No matter how much they tried, they still had thoughts. Some say they're not able to "clear" their minds.

Let's take that last one on first. If your mind is clear, it means you are dead. Golf is hard enough without being dead. Your mind is always focused on something. That is natural; that's what your mind does. Your mind is a thinking machine. It exists to think. If you are thinking, you are alive and healthy.

Secondly, you cannot be a bad meditator. Most people say they cannot stay focused on anything for more than a few seconds. That's good news! It means you are a human being with a mind, and exceedingly normal.

Meditation is not about controlling your thoughts. No matter how much we might try to stop thinking about something, we cannot control our thoughts. They just keep on coming. If, for

---

[3] I believe that personal accountability is crucial to living consciously. My favourite definition of accountability comes from the ManKind Project: "I am 100 per cent responsible for my actions and their consequences, intended or unintended." That may seem over the top, but I figure that degree of responsibility keeps me conscious and moving in the direction that I've chosen for myself. Accountability is a foundational attribute of self-governance for executing on your commitments to yourself and others. This topic is worthy of its own book.)

example, you're worried about screwing up down the stretch of a tournament, that's normal. However, you can choose how to respond to your thoughts, and shift your attention to something that serves you in the moment.

You could, for example, look intently at your surroundings, feel your feet as you walk, listen closely to your fellow competitors, feel the breeze on your face, smell the fresh-cut grass, and so on. Through mediation, you develop the skill of awareness about what your mind is doing, which allows you to choose a response that serves you.

You might find this odd, especially for a book aimed at golf nerds, but meditation is not about staying focused, being calm and relaxed, lowering your heart rate, and so on. Those are all lovely bonuses that you receive from meditation, and there's no doubt in my mind that meditation can improve your golf game.

But mainly, meditation is the practice of being aware. Rather than being jerked around by your mind and repeating self-sabotaging behaviours, you will develop awareness of what you are thinking and feeling which dictate your behaviours. You will have more clarity and perspective. Rather than be hijacked, you have an opportunity to discern what you consciously want to do.

That alone will make a difference in your golf and in your life.

As a golf nerd, you desire to be better. However, I suggest you aim higher. Being "better" is based on the past, which keeps you tied to old behaviours that your ego has created as part of your false self, the one that keeps you stuck.

Why not create a new future by becoming your true self? I know that sounds way mystical, but it's your egoic false self that keeps you frustrated in your golf and your life. It keeps you searching outside of yourself for solutions, fixes, and happiness, and yet leaves you unsatisfied and forever seeking.

This next bit is completely counter-intuitive to the messages you get in our golf and wider culture, but ... you are whole and complete. You have everything you need within you. You do not need fixing.

Your golf swing, your ability to gauge distances, and your creative touch are all within you. As a consequence of being a human, you have incredible gifts and innate wisdom that has been developed over millions of years of evolution. These are the gifts of your true self.

Your challenge is to draw them out and use them to develop your skills. To break from your false self requires transformation. It's not easy. Most truly transformative moments result from hard lessons. But we can facilitate our transformation through practices such as mediation.

All transformation starts with awareness. No awareness, no transformation.

GUIDELINES FOR MEDITATION

If you want to try meditation, here are guidelines for a simple practice:

- Find a quiet place.
- Set a timer for two or three minutes.[4]
- Sit up straight with your feet on the floor, hands on your thighs. Tuck in your chin.[5]
- Close your eyes. (Some people like to leave their eyes open and fix their gaze on the floor or a wall.)
- Allow your attention to settle on your breathing. (You don't need to do anything but allow yourself to breathe.)[6]
- Allow your attention to focus on any aspect of your breathing:
  - It could be the feeling of the air coming in and out of our nose.

[4]Two or three minutes may seem short, but for novice meditators it can feel like an eternity.

[5]If you can sit in the lotus position, or kneel using a meditation bench, go for it. But sitting in a chair—provided you're not leaning back—is fine.

[6]It is relatively easy to focus on our breath because it's continuous, and it happens independently—if you let it. I don't advocate counting your breaths or deliberately breathing in through the nose and exhaling through the mouth. (If that works for you, fine.) It's my sense, certainly for novices, that we experience freedom in allowing the breath to happen on its own. Most golfers have spent a lifetime trying to control things. My invitation is to let your breath be. For many people, just allowing is a risk to release control, trust, and surrender to the wisdom, power, and brilliance of the body. Your role is simply to observe your breath, and you can do that by feeling it and listening to it. (Heck, in cold weather, you can observe it!)

- – Or the sound of your breath.
  - – Or the feeling of your chest and stomach moving.
  - – Or whatever interests you.
- Make it your intention to focus on your breathing for the time you've allotted.
- When you notice that your attention has drifted to thinking, simply re-focus on your breath.

MEETING YOUR MONKEY MIND

Despite your intention to focus on our breathing, your mind *will* inevitably drift into thinking. Over and over again. It's natural. But when you find yourself thinking during meditation, it doesn't mean you are doing it wrong. You have not proven that you're bad at it. You've proven your humanity. There's no need to judge yourself.

When you become aware that you are thinking, here's what you do: simply bring your attention back to your breathing. That's it. But as sure as the sun comes up every morning, your mind will drift into thinking again and again and again. When you become conscious that you're thinking, simply return your attention to your breathing.

Repeat. Repeat. Repeat.

You will have rare days when you find it relatively easily to stay focused on your breath. And there will be days when your mind flits into thinking every few seconds; it usually means you have some important things that are calling for your attention. As a therapist friend of mine says, "When your basement is filling up with water, you better pay attention to it."

If you continue to practice meditation, you will begin to notice what your mind is doing more quickly. You will notice, "Oh, I'm thinking." And you will bring your focus back to your breath. Doing this very simple practice on a frequent, if not daily basis, will gradually build your skill of awareness. Your mindfulness muscles will grow and become more acute, and kick in more quickly.

HERE'S HOW MEDITATION CAN HELP YOUR GOLF

When you can't find a fairway or make a putt, rather searching through your mental files for a corrective swing thought, you will notice: "Oh, I'm searching for a fix again." And you'll realize you have a choice about where to place your attention.

Rather than think, you could focus on your breathing or feel what's happening in your body. The feeling brain is stronger and far wiser than the thinking brain. You might discover that you're tense, walking and talking quickly, swinging fast, or even too slowly and carefully.

You can call upon your skill of awareness when, for example, you realize you are worrying about keeping a good round going, ruminating about your last three-putt, or how your wedges keep misbehaving. In that space, you have the power to choose your response.

Highly aware people excel in their fields because they have a higher sense of awareness; their awareness is sharp and kicks in quickly. They also tend to be less prone to becoming emotionally upset, distracted, and frustrated.

To get you started, I invite you to commit to three two- to

three-minute meditation sessions over the next week. In the following weeks, experiment with sitting for four, five and eventually seven days a week.[7]

After you've been mediating for a while—the duration is different for everyone—you will likely find that two or three minutes are tolerable. Increase your time to, say, four or five minutes. As you develop your practice, challenge yourself to sit longer. For most people, 10 minutes is quite sufficient and easy to slot into their day. If you can sit for longer, terrific, but 10 minutes is fine.

Don't confine your meditation to a sitting practice. Take it on the course and into your life. I call it meditation on the run. That is, practice meditation when you're on a tee box, on a green, walking to the first tee, sitting in a waiting room, in line at the grocery store, on a plane, in a slow-moving drive-through line. You don't need to close your eyes. Simply pay attention to something that interests you. You will be surprised at how your mind slows down, your worries decrease in intensity, and you feel more at home in your body.

Meditation means many things to many people, but for golfers seeking to increase their sense of awareness of their thinking and their emotions, it is a valuable and practical practice.

---

[7] The following is a great mindfulness practice: When you are eating, don't look at your phone or a screen, read a book or magazine, or listen to music or a podcast. Your intention is to just "be with" your food; to notice the difference when you are fully in the experience of eating, rather than being distracted. You may be surprised by how good your food really tastes, and that you eat less.

THE HALLOWED PRESENT MOMENT

Meditation allows us to experience the present moment, which is a rarity for most of us. We are conditioned to always be thinking.

Our thoughts are always about the future or the past. The brain is constantly scanning for future threats and working to prevent painful events from happening again. The brain does this because its No. 1 job is to keep us alive.

When we're in the present moment, we are not thinking. There's nothing to process, calibrate, judge, weigh, rehearse, seek, and on and on. When we're present, it's more like our minds are just *with* whatever is happening. Our minds are drinking in what's happening, absorbing, feeling.

Even though our minds default to thinking about the future or the past, we're always in the present moment. This may sound contradictory, but as Fred Shoemaker eloquently said: "It's always now." He explained that when you are thinking about the future, it's like a fantasy from where you are right now. When you remember something from the past, it's a memory from where you are now.

Yet, we're rarely here now.

The concept of "being present" can be difficult to understand. It's a challenge because our minds are conditioned not to be present. It's easy to blame our attachment to our phones, social media, et al., but being distracted and constantly lost in thought is how most people have conditioned their minds.

This explains why the idea of being present seems strange

and almost unnatural to many people.[8]

Rather than intellectualize about what it means to be present, it's much easier to experience it. The simplest way to experience presence is by connecting with the breath, which explains why the most popular form of meditation is Vipassana, in which you focus on your breath. The constancy of your breath, the sound of your breath, and even the way it makes your body move, makes it the easiest of your senses to connect with.

The mind is constantly flitting into the future or the past, but our bodily senses are always in the present moment. Your body doesn't time travel. Technology has made many things possible that we couldn't have imagined 10 or 20 years ago, but so far, we still can't do that "Beam me up Scotty" thing portrayed on *Star Trek*.

When you are focused on the breath, you're not analyzing, judging, comparing, questioning, complaining, searching, cogitating, solving, and all the many things that our minds do. It's like you're just hanging out with your breath, riding along for each inhalation and exhalation, and the pauses in between. Your mind is quiet.

You can focus on your breathing during a formal sit, but also anywhere—walking in the fairway, watching your partners putt—for as little or as long as you want. And no one will know you're focused on your breath.

---

[8]To make the concept of being present easier for golfers to understand, PGA of America Professional Susie Meyers came up with the wonderful idea: play every shot from Point A. You're not focused on future or past shots. Meyers said Point A is much easier to understand than adages such as "play one shot at a time." I highly recommend her book *Golf From Point A*.

Of course, the breath is just one of our senses. A golf course is a wonderful place to practice being present. There's so much for our senses to savour. It could be the sensation of a wedge gently swaying back and then descending through the ball, and the feeling of the wrists hinging and releasing. Or the warm breeze on your cheek, the sweet fragrance of wildflowers, or birds participating in a call-and-response songfest. Or a warm taste of coffee on a cool morning or watching the leaves shimmer on an oak tree in the breeze.

At these moments—when we're engaging with the world through our senses—the mind is connected to something real and wonderful like a golf course. It doesn't get much better for a golf nerd.

It could be a silhouette of a loved one that silences you and stops you in your tracks. You might even remember a time when you felt suspended from the hubbub of your life, and that whatever was happening was good, simple, and perhaps even amazing.[9]

And you might even find yourself whispering "wow" or "thanks." To me, those rare moments of presence sustain me through the nonsense of the way my mind habitually works. I consider them hallowed moments when I feel a profound connection to something greater than my golf score.

---

[9]This may alienate some folks, but I love the combined fragrance of fresh-cut grass and gasoline. I'm instantly transported back to caddying and playing golf as a junior on sunlit, summer mornings at Sunningdale G&CC, my parents' club in London, Ontario.

- Commit to three meditation sessions of two to three minutes over the next week. In the following weeks, gradually increase the time and experiment with sitting for four, five and eventually seven days a week.

- When you are eating, focus only on your food. Don't look at screens, books, magazines, or listen to anything. Your intention is to just "be with" your food and notice the difference between when you are fully in the experience of eating and being distracted.

- When you go for walks around your neighbourhood and when you're on a golf course, focus on your sensations. Just witness what you are feeling or experiencing.

The value of asking "Why do I play golf?"

Like many golfers of a certain vintage, I was introduced to golf by my late father as both a sport and a way to make money. Back in the day at private clubs like Sunningdale Golf & Country Club in London, Ontario, it was possible for kids as young as 10 or so to caddie.

My father Dennis was an affable fellow and a pretty good player at Sunningdale, where he got down to about a six handicap at his best. Dad could talk with anyone. When he got laid off from the railroad in his early twenties, he asked his older brother John what he should do. John said: "You're full of shit. Sell insurance."

He did. And Dad was very good at it, which made it possible for our family to belong to Sunningdale.

I became an avid junior golfer, but I was a far better caddie than a player. Due to dear old Dad's influence, I was thoroughly schooled in the noble art of course etiquette, and I kept my player's clubs and golf ball clean at all times. I could talk without fear with adults, yet I also knew when to keep my ears open and my mouth shut.

The best players at the club asked me to caddie for them in the club championship and big club events at Sunningdale. Caddying for scratch players in competitions was exciting; I believe those experiences are among the key reasons that golf got its hooks in me.

As I got older and began taking a hard look at my life, I determined that I believed my worth as a man was equated with my performance. That manifested itself in my desire to be a low-handicap player and to show off a technically proficient swing that would cause heads to turn. But that intense desire to impress and be a "player" like the scratch golfers that I caddied for as a kid caused me to become a paralysis-by-analysis basket-case—a frustrated, underachieving wanna-be.[1]

In my efforts to find some more freedom and improve my game, I became a devotee of Fred Shoemaker and started doing a number of exercises that he recommended, including a writing exercise that I called Why Do I Play Golf.

In writing my "why," it came back to me that golf has always been a key part of my connection with my parents. My mother Margaret was an avid player too; I enjoyed games in which it was just the two of us. I felt relaxed with Mom because I knew there would be zero commentary on the state of my putting stroke, which was a hazard of golf with Dad.

---

[1] My self-worth was also caught up in how well I played bass guitar, in the quality of the magazines that published me, with the car I drove, and how much money I made, yada yada.

I was excited to return to Sunningdale as a young adult a few times a season to play on a Saturday morning with Dad and his golf buddies. I was always nervous; anxious to show him and his pals—to whom he bragged about his son, the golf writer—that I was indeed a player. I was so tight you couldn't ram a nail up my butt with a hammer. I rode an emotional roller coaster, and usually choked my guts out. I'm embarrassed to admit it, but I often sulked and dragged my carcass around the course like I was headed to the gallows.

As a young man, I didn't have the perspective that while my father certainly hoped I'd play well, for him it was mainly about sharing time, Sunningdale and the game we loved. Talk about if-I-knew-then-what-I-know-now perspective.

More than a few times, Dad would say early in the back nine, "Hey pal, let's have fun." Being an arrogant know-it-all whipper-snapper, I would dismiss this as more of his unwanted fatherly advice. I thought: "For God's sake, I write about the game! I interview PGA Tour players and coaches!" When I continued to play with painstaking deliberateness only to hit the ball into oblivion, he'd sometimes say, "Let's see your 'Don't-give-a-shit swing.'" Fuming, and with nothing to lose, I'd swing away freely and—pretty well every freaking time—nail a beauty straight down the pike. I think Dad's don't-give-a-shit-swing suggestion was a crude forerunner of "stay out of your own way."

It wasn't until my boys were playing sports that I realized what was really important. The gift of playing golf with my Dad was being together, connecting, walking in the sunshine in a beautiful place, relishing his golf aphorisms, sharing observations about the game, or recounting what happened in last week's pro tournament.

When we were both older, I had zero expectations for my own game when we played together. My only intention was to enjoy our shared time together playing the game we loved. Writing out Why Do I Play Golf reminded me that I play golf for connection, especially to memories and feelings associated with playing with Mom and Dad, but also with my golf buddies both on the course and off.

The writing practice also affirmed that my Why certainly includes my desire to be a "player," and that when I commit to swinging like I don't give a shit, I can play some nice golf. Thanks Dad.

Determining Where You're Going … and How to Get There

As golf nerds, we can get bent *way* out of shape. It's easy to find ourselves angry, sulking, brooding, and behaving like a five-year-old having a temper tantrum, as per my reaction to my four-putt in my club championship. We know it's foolish, but we do it anyway. My favourite coaster in our house says: "A well-adjusted person is one who can play golf as if it were a game."

We all get plenty of irritating advice, especially to "think positively." These kinds of bromides are part of a self-help culture that promises that if you do the right things, you'll be happy. No wonder so many people are miserable.

Golf culture lures you in by promising that if you "get better," you'll finally be happy. Not true. I've met several touring pros and plus-handicap golfers who are self-absorbed cranks who remind me of a bylaw officer inspecting your new fence for a design violation.

According to golf culture, "good golfers" are supposed to have ascended to sublime levels of happiness. I've been awaiting to ascend for about 40 years, but I still find myself fighting the occasional impulse to helicopter a misbehaving putter into a pond.

As humans, we get triggered. We find ourselves deep in rabbit holes of circular thinking and feelings of confusion and even despair, sometimes for days, weeks or even a season. There are many aspirational junior and college-aged golfers and touring pros who suffer to the point they suffer mental breakdowns. Some feel like they have failed to fulfil their own hopes, and the potential that others saw in them. Some suffer horridly and fall out of love with the game or into addiction.

Some go into therapy to start some healing. Unfortunately, many will not seek help; they try to battle on their own. They consider it a sign of weakness or that they might be labelled. Some golfers take a break from the game. Some abandon their quest; high-level golf is not for everyone. I've coached some young professionals who stopped playing competitively for the good of their overall health.

It's not uncommon to hear an amateur golfer say, "I'm glad that I don't rely on my golf to make a living." I am gobsmacked by the courage of many touring pros who keep their dream alive on the developmental tours despite the financial uncertainty and the strain on their relationships. There are many parallels, such as musicians who grind out 300 gigs a year, the solo entrepreneur, or the commission-only salesperson.

Amateur golfers don't face these financial pressures, but we often act as if our homes and identities were on the line. It's ridiculous. But I don't care if you're the Dalai Lama or Eckhart

Tolle, if you have golf in your soul, this game is going to piss you off and torture you.

As I've experienced throughout my life as a player and a coach, it's easy to get tossed about on the stormy seas of our expectations and cravings and get thrown off course. I am constantly asked, "How do I shut all the noise off in my head?" "How do I get out of these cycles of bad golf?"

It's not from perfecting your backswing. I've been down that road. My experience is that golfers have more fun, suffer fewer meltdowns and move forward when they have a strong vision for themselves—when they've determined what's truly important to them, where they are going, and how to get there.

If you're going to move forward consciously in your golf and life—whether you're a passionate once-a-week player or a tour professional—you must have a mission.

Of course, most people don't, never have and never will. But let me ask: Do you want to drift through life or choose your path?

Without a mission, I argue that you'll be perennially dissatisfied. Without a mission, you're prone to trying anything when your golf goes south. This constant seeking keeps you in a chronic state of disequilibrium, disconnection from your body, and seeking for answers outside of your own experience. This is the path of mediocrity, unhappiness, and dissatisfaction that many golfers experience.

A mission articulates and identifies your higher purpose. A mission serves as your personal lighthouse. When you are tossed around by your inevitable stumbles, slumps and disappointments, your mission or higher purpose keeps you moving toward your destination, where you want to go with your golf.

Having a mission gives meaning to your life—to acquire what well-known golf nerd Aristotle called "eudaimonia," a life well-lived with a sense of purpose and virtue. Social scientist Timothy D. Wilson writes that a mission provides us with a good narrative. "People who have such a narrative—who feel in control of their lives, have goals of their own choosing, and make progress toward those goals—are happier than people who do not … The important thing is to pursue goals that give us a sense of autonomy, effectiveness, and mastery."[1]

Having a higher purpose is a crucial factor for being more resilient to stress, according to a 2007 research paper on highly resilient individuals titled "6 Keys to Resilience for PTSD and Everyday Stress."[2]

The authors noted that a higher purpose allows you to focus on what is essential rather than being distracted by circumstances. For a golfer, these could include as a flubbed shot, a few bad holes, an annoying partner, or an angry spouse or cranky co-worker. A higher purpose sets your priorities for how you choose to act.

For example, a higher purpose for a golf season could be in a one-line statement such as:

- "I am committed to learning how to hit my irons solidly."
- "My intention is to stay focused on feeling athletic."
- "I accept wherever the ball goes."

[1] Timothy D. Wilson. *Redirect: The Surprising New Science of Psychological Change.* Little Brown. Page 69.
[2] Search for Semantic Scholar: 6 Keys to Resilience for PTSD published by M. Haglund, N. Cooper and D Charney in April 2007.

- "I play with creativity and freedom."
- "I am not defined by my golf scores; I'm dedicated to following my process."
- "I am committed to the plan that my coach and I have worked out."
- "My focus is always on the shot that I face; never in the future, nor the past."

(These are merely suggestions; you will determine your own. As we'll see, your mission or paradigm can be one sentence, a few sentences, or longer. It's up to you. Like meditation, there's no right or wrong way to do it.)

There is a lot of power in having an intention. I generally think of an intention as a guide for the round. When you are committed to an intention, it puts things in perspective and keeps you focused on what's truly important to you that day. For example, your intent could be "Today is about having fun with my Dad," or "I'm focused on being a great host for my client."

Having a higher purpose can act like a mantra that you repeat to yourself before and during a round. Many golfers write their mission or paradigm on their scorecard or in their yardage books so they are reminded throughout their round. Setting an intention gives you a higher purpose for a specific round of golf, such as "I am focused on playing my own game today" or "I am a great partner." It doesn't need to be more complicated than that. (There's more about intention in the "Intervention" interlude.)

Without a mission, it's far too easy to become embroiled in your personal drama, and grasp at any shiny nugget that promises instant salvation. This keeps you chained to your past behaviours, caught in your stories, and succumbing to the non-stop thoughts pinging around your noggin.

The most resilient golfers are firmly grounded with a sense of purpose. As of this writing, Scottie Scheffler has just won his second Masters in three years, and six of his last 10 tournaments. While Scheffler talks about how much he cares about winning, the foundations of his life since he was a child are family and faith. With that solid grounding, I believe that he's not as prone to a racing mind or roller-coaster emotions.

It's also my belief that Jordan Spieth survives the mercurial ups and downs of professional golf because of his family's focus on his sister Ellie. When Jordan was growing up, the family rallied around taking care of his special needs sister. "Ellie keeps things normal," Rosalind Funderburgh, the founder of Ellie's school, told *Golf Digest*. This speaks to being part of something bigger than ourselves.

One of my most memorable interviews as a golfer writer was with the late Bruce Lietzke, who won 13 events on the PGA Tour, and seven on the Champions Tour. He was not colourful or charismatic, the average fan was barely aware of him, and he didn't have a swing that anyone would emulate—he played a plodding game with his slightly over-the-top swing that hit a fade that was as reliable as the earth rotates around the sun.

Lietzke told me that his reason for playing professional golf was simple: it allowed him the freedom to be an attentive father and spouse, coach his son and daughter in baseball, fish and restore cars. His dedication to his family was his "why" for playing golf. He found meaning and purpose in his family that put golf clearly in its place.

That commitment also kept him from experimenting with his one-dimensional swing. He saw no reason to tinker with his swing to "take his game to the next level" or, say, draw the ball right to left to make him better suited to Augusta National. He had one equipment company over 27 years (Tommy Armour), one teacher (his brother Duane), and no agent after 1985.[3]

Lietzke's commitment to his vision gave him a "What, me worry?" vibe and humbleness that I found endearing. He struck me as a grounded man who lived according to strong values and principles. When I think about people to emulate in the world, Bruce Lietzke has always been near the top of my list.[4]

Every golf nerd I ever met wants to hit better shots. We want to shoot lower scores, decrease our index, become grittier in competition, and some are driven to win tournaments.

However, here are some questions to ask yourself: What's my motivation? Is it to look good, be recognized, and validated? Or feel self-satisfaction, do some self-exploration, and feel joy? The former is extrinsic, about how others see and judge us; the latter is intrinsic, about self-discovery. There's nothing wrong with external motivation, but it can cause golf nerds to get crazy. It's worth looking at what we're really after.

---

[3] Jeff Rude. "Remembering Bruce Lietzke: A funny, friendly family man, gone too soon." GOLF Magazine. https://golf.com/news/remembering-bruce-lietzke/

[4] The banana story bolsters Lietzke's approach to life. At the conclusion of one season in the 1980s, he told caddie Al Hansen that he wouldn't touch his clubs until the Bob Hope tournament in the New Year. Hansen didn't believe him, so he stuck a banana in the driver headcover. When they unzipped the travel bag in January, it was a disgusting, smelly mess.

When we're guided extrinsically, we're prone to being pulled and shoved around by our compulsions, feelings of inadequacy, confusion, and often helplessness.

We all want to feel good and know that we're going to be OK no matter how dark it may get. That's an inside job. We're talking about inspiration. That is, what is springing forth from inside you that reveals your innate talents, your unique traits, and gifts—your true self—rather than motivating external factors.

It's not easy to stay true to your own inner compass, but I believe it's possible when you have a mission for playing the game that is grounded on things that are both bigger than yourself and connected to your spirit.

MISSION = VISION + ACTION

When you determine your mission as a golfer and commit to it, it becomes your focus. Yes, you want the mission to deliver the results you desire, but your focus is not on results—it's always on the mission, your higher purpose, your path.

Your mission provides you with direction, clarity, and resolve. It also helps prevent you from succumbing to your compulsions and addiction to results.

A mission can appear simple and humble like Lietzke's, or grand in scope, perhaps even crazy in its reach. But bringing that vision into reality requires action. You don't accomplish anything in this world by thinking or talking about it. It's through action in whatever you do—as a golfer, parent, spouse, businessperson, anyone. I like the metaphor for action used by marketing guru Seth Godin: you must ship your work.

Mission comprises two essential elements: vision and action. Following a mission is making a commitment to the vision and the actions that will bring it to fruition. "Action without vision is only passing time; vision without action is merely day dreaming, but vision with action can change the world," Nelson Mandela said.

Now there's a formula for a fulfilling life.

Here's my mission as a coach: "As a compassionate and intentional man, I create a world where people can be their true selves." Through the actions of being a compassionate and intentional man, I bring my vision to fruition by creating a world—you could say experiences, space, or opportunities—where people can discover their true selves.

Here are some more examples of a mission, combining visions and action:

- As a golfer dedicated to excellence and resilience, I always follow my practice plan.
- To reach my goal of breaking 120 (110, 100, 90, 80), I am taking lessons and remain focused on what my coach and I agree to work on.
- To make myself more competitive, I play from the back tees once a week and putt everything out.
- To improve my short game, I spend 75 per cent of my practice time in the short-game area and have a weekly one-hour short-game practice session in my calendar.
- I calm myself and quiet my mind by focusing on my breathing on every tee box and savouring the beauty of the golf course.

- My ideal round is to be grateful for purely struck shots and my partners.

As per earlier in this chapter, these are merely examples of a mission that a player could have for a month, a season, or longer. (The next chapter will provide you with a process for exploring and discovering the key elements that could make up your mission.)

Notice how these are all worded in the present tense as actions you are taking now, rather than things to be done in the future. This is a key piece in making commitments.

Some people create what's known as a paradigm, which serves as their governing model. A paradigm is a model or program that governs your habitual behaviours. As we've discussed, almost all of your behaviour is habitual. "Paradigms are the way you view yourself, the world, and opportunity," writes Sandy Gallagher in *Change Your Paradigm, Change Your Life* by Bob Proctor.

Here are some examples of possible paradigms:

- Every round is an opportunity to learn more about myself.
- Golf allows me to discover what I'm capable of and what's possible for me.
- Everything that happens to me on a golf course makes me stronger.
- Golf is an act of creation that cannot be measured or critiqued.
- Whether I shoot low or high scores, they have no bearing on my self-worth and identity.
- Golf allows me to tap into my innate brilliance, creativity, and athleticism.

Within a paradigm, there are values and practices that constitute a way of self-regulating oneself in the world. Your paradigm is your way of being. It is not entered into lightly or tried on like a set of clothes.

Your mission or your paradigm is not about controlling yourself, staying strong, or having willpower, and so on. But a golfer who is committed to self-discovery and forging an intentional path isn't a dabbler, tinkerer, or a compulsive slave to their desires. A golfer with a mission or defined paradigm has honestly reflected on their past actions and behaviours and taken 100 per cent responsibility for their golf. They have defined the future that they want to live in.

This speaks to the irony that commitment is freeing. When you commit, you are free from rationalization, excuses, and temptation when confronted with the inevitable triggers, distractions, and hills and valleys of hope and despair that golfers traverse. A mission or paradigm provides the structure that Fred Shoemaker referred to when he told me, "The only freedom that I found in golf was through a structure, and the only freedom I've found was through a commitment."

Staying on your path requires committing to something solid and unshakable, taking action, and holding yourself accountable.

So how do you find your mission? What is the process of determining your mission and then committing to it? What can keep you from being chained to our past?

I believe it can start by asking yourself the question: Why do I play golf?

Do the Why Do I Play Golf exercise, and then come back to this chapter and start drafting your mission.

"Oh my God. I killed my driver!"

Just about every golf nerd who has kids discovers that the game takes a backseat to family. If you don't, you risk moving into a bachelor apartment where the hallway smells like cat pee.

Once Sandy and I had our two boys, it became almost impossible to schedule a game with both my parents and my brother Pat on a weekend. One summer during my consultant years, we arranged a weekday game. We got the first tee time of the day.

On arrival at Sunningdale, I became a little nervous, remembering that when you're first off the tee, you're expected to play briskly to set a good pace for the day. During my warm-up, I hit a few shanks, an affliction that had recently infected my game, ramping up my pre-game heebie-jeebies.

Soon after teeing off, I noticed that we were followed by "rabbits." Every private club has them; the foursome of retired guys whose grand ambition is to play in a faster time than the day before. I don't understand it, but I'm thinking it's some kind of masculine impulse about getting shit done; I think it also replaces the dopamine hit they used to get when they were working and telling people what to do.

From the get-go, the rabbits were on our tails, waiting in the fairway with their hands on their hips or their arms folded— the usual passive-aggressive signals that waiting golfers send to the group ahead to indicate their impatience.

Looking back at them, I could feel myself tightening up. I walked and talked faster and told my parents and Pat that we'd better get going. Uncharacteristically for Dad, who was always skittish about holding anyone up, he said: "Don't worry about it. We're having a family game. We're doing all right."

I had so wanted this game to be a lovely stroll down the hallowed fairways of Sunningdale where I shared many great memories with my parents and Pat. This was supposed to be the golf equivalent of a Hallmark Christmas movie where Dad tousles my hair to show his pride that he raised a killer golfer, Mom kisses me for a great putt, and Pat and I exchange high fives after monster drives.

With every hole, I became increasingly agitated, and my game was quickly going south. The golf author and consultant was a hacking, miserable, pouting, sulking, silent, fast-walking brat.

As we got to the par-three sixth tee, I suggested we let the rabbits play through. Dad and Pat initially didn't like the idea; allowing a foursome of fellow members to play through seems unmanly, like an admission of weakness. The foursome briskly hit their shots as we stood in grumpy silence. My mother looked at me and rolled her eyes. She had seen this movie before.

Feeling somewhat relieved on the next hole, I hit a solid drive that left a wedge to the green. I swung. The ball veered dead right. A shank! Not @#$%^& now! I trudged over to the ball which had settled in a rat's nest of broadleaf weeds.

I swung my wedge again. Fuck! Another @#$%^& shank! The ball disappeared down a hillside of thigh-high weeds.

My world went black. I swung the business end of the wedge at my golf stand bag. I heard a strange cracking sound. Something was happening to the head cover of my driver. Then it slowly and sickeningly tipped forward like an elderly person having a fainting spell and fell to the ground.

Oh my God! I killed my driver! My fucking $600 driver! I committed an act of gross violence. I was that worst kind of golfer who can't control his impulses. I was that guy! Even worse, I had committed this mortal sin while playing with my loving parents —at Sunningdale!—with my younger brother witnessing his older brother completely lose his shit.

The driver head—still ensconced in its leather head cover— had been on the ground about a millisecond when I grabbed it with my right hand while undoing the zipper on the side of the bag with my left and stuffed it inside to hide the evidence. Oh, the shame!

I spiraled into a raging meltdown. Taking giant steps, I hurtled to the eighth tee, where I frantically paced around in circles, simultaneously beating the living crap out of myself, and debating whether I should drive home right there and then. My chest was heaving, my face ran with sweat, my mind raced.

When my parents and Pat walked on to the tee, I wasn't sure what anyone was going to say. "Hey Tim, we missed you," Dad said, with a mischievous smile that telegraphed he was certainly aware of my little freak-out.

As I had with all my major emotional moments, I went straight to Mom. If I locked on her blue eyes, I could always eke out some words. I fessed up to the violence. With a faint smile, she said, "That's OK. We all do stupid things from time to time." That was Mom, comforting but not one to shirk from the truth.

And with that, the craziness started to drain away. Of course, I was going to stay. I was last to hit off the tee—with my three-wood—and I purposely took my time so I could walk behind them down the fairway.

As I walked, I thought about the objective of the day—to savour my time with my parents and Pat, regardless of rabbits or the quality of my game. My parents didn't care how I played. They were happy we were together playing the game we loved at the course we loved. It was about connecting, having fun, and being thankful for that blessing.

The rest of the game was everything that I had hoped it would be—my Hallmark family golf movie.

By the way, on the back nine I shot 39. Breaking 40 was always important to me. On this day, it was the least important thing.

Why Do I Play Golf?

When I start working with most of my new coaching clients, I ask them to do a writing exercise. The exercise starts with the golfer writing "Why Do I Play Golf" across the top of a piece of paper. Then they answer the question.

You might respond that you already know "why." But I'll bet that if you immerse yourself in the exercise, you'll be surprised by what you discover.

Why I play golf is a great question to ponder or talk about with a friend. But I believe that just thinking and talking won't lead you to the deeper truth you're seeking. When we think, we're liable to stay stuck in our ego-mind: it's like there's a tennis match between new ideas and our old stories; the possibilities of an uncertain future are met with the resistances of the past.

You could talk with a friend but it's my sense that we're often self-conscious about what we say and how someone will react, so we self-edit and don't get down into what's real.

As a writer, I have a bias toward writing as a tool of self-discovery, healing, and developing perspective, but social psychologists also recognize its value. Organizational psychologist

Adam Grant says: "Turning thoughts into words sharpens reasoning. What is fuzzy in your head is clear on the page." I believe that writing is one of the best ways to improve your relationship with the game and establish your mission or paradigm.

I suggest you start by getting a spiral notebook with 8½ x 11 paper and a pen that has excellent flow. If you like, you can customize your notebook with pictures, drawings, doodles, add commentary in the margins, and so on. I believe that longhand is ideal because writing is a mind-body experience. This may just be a prejudice, but I also think that words on a page are more tangible and durable than on a screen. When they go down on the page, they're irreversible—that's unless you cross them out, which I implore you to resist. (More on this in a moment.)

However, if you prefer to type on a computer, that's fine, especially if you find it easier to transmit your thoughts through your fingers and record them more quickly. Some people may prefer to record their voice, which is also fine. My hesitation with audio is that it's not as easy to review what you've recorded as writing, but if that works for you, go for it!

You'll need about 20 minutes. It's best to do this exercise when you're relatively fresh and you won't be interrupted. I find the ideal time is first thing in the morning before I've looked online or talked to anyone. If that's not possible before doing the exercise, do your best to avoid scrolling on your phone or checking email, all of which elevates your brain waves and promotes ego-centric thinking.

The key is to start writing and keep going until you are finished three full pages. Don't stop to correct grammar or spelling, think, look out the window for inspiration, or look for ideas from the internet. Don't try to write well.

If you are typing, just keeping typing, getting words down. Don't use the delete button, or backspace to correct mistakes.

Try not to judge the quality of your writing, whether it's "deep," or any good. You could even write "I don't know what to write," or repeat what you've written before. If you judge yourself as not having good ideas or "I'm not a very good writer," write that down. Just keep going. Write whatever comes into your mind. It's all good to go on the page. No one is going to read this except you, so there's no reason to hold back on anything.

The key is to keep writing continuously. This exercise is designed so that you can plunge 100 per cent into what is true for you: your experiences, feelings, what's important, and perhaps memories that you haven't recalled for years, even decades. Allow whatever's inside you to spill on to the page.

Writing in this free-flowing way allows you to get below your ego-mind and into your subconscious.[1] That's where the good stuff is. When you stop thinking and let the pen flow, the words just seem to accumulate on the page. It's like those rare and lovely episodes in golf where we feel like we're in The Zone.

Keep writing until you fill all three pages and stop. If you are typing, stop when you've typed about 800 words. (There are about 250 handwritten words per page.) If you feel like you've

---

[1] This kind of writing was popularized by writer and coach Julia Cameron who described the process as Morning Pages. Her classic book, *The Artist's Way* is an excellent resource on fostering creativity, self discovery, and overcoming resistance.

just opened the flood gates, keep writing; you're not beholden to three pages. The intention of setting a goal of three pages is to provide space to drop into your subconscious and keep going. Three pages is a stretch for most people while others have just warmed up.[2]

When you are done, put it away. Don't look at what you wrote until later in the day, or until the next day. When you've finished, it's not unusual to feel some emotion; you might feel a little raw, sad, or even joyful. In that state, you may feel the need to refine, correct or elaborate on some things. Instead, just let it be. You've allowed yourself to expressly yourself freely, which is a new experience for many people. Allow yourself to have that experience, rather than concern yourself if you did it right or your writing meets any kind of standard.

When you read it, I'll bet that you'll find it interesting, perhaps even fascinating. You may be surprised by the emotions you feel. Most people who do this exercise are surprised. (If you enjoy this kind of free writing, you will find it's valuable for generating ideas, brainstorming, and working through problems as you'll see in an upcoming chapter.)

When golfers do the exercise, it's not uncommon that they'll write that they're competitive, "I want to reach my potential," lower their index, or break a scoring barrier—the kinds of things that golfers often say when they're asked why they play golf. This is not to judge that these are shallow or misguided notions, but they are often the first things that come to mind. This is what

---

[2]The late, great golf writer Herbert Warren Wind once joked he needed 5,000 words just to clear his throat.

most golfers fixate on. It's ingrained in golf culture, and it's an unconscious pattern that many of us follow.

However, as most people continue writing, they go deeper; they are often reminded of great times with their parents, of specific moments or places, of times when they felt very happy and connected to friends. You might reconnect with how golf provides you with a sense of escape from your work and worries. You may remember a time when you laughed yourself silly, or a scene that mesmerized you. Or a time you had a specific insight or learned an important lesson.

What people write about runs the gamut. Your written account of your "why" is as unique to you as your fingerprints, and a window into your head, heart, and soul. You may connect with feelings and insights that are quite different from the usual things that you focus on when you play golf.

Interestingly, most of the feelings, recollections, and reflections that come up have little to do with solving a swing flaw or shooting low scores. Rather than focusing on our "usual game," we're on a higher plane of consciousness. Note that a higher plane doesn't mean better or superior, just different, as if we were in a new space. This higher plane is a place of perspective, not unlike when we go to a funeral or have a health crisis; we gain perspective about what's "important."

Some of the things you write might make you feel sentimental, joyful, or even embarrassed, but they are all integral parts of your golf journey. You are writing about these things because they are part of your relationship to golf and yourself.

(At the end of this chapter, I've included some examples of what people have written about their "why.")

I've done this exercise count-less times, and it comes up all the time that I seek to play golf with a greater sense of freedom, which is what I've been striving for in other parts of my life.

Rather than be a careful person who feels inadequate and compelled to meet some kind of standard, I have sought to play golf freely and instinctively—my way. My why has also included several things—connection with my mother and father, with my sons, as well as savouring the adventure of a round of golf, escaping into a world of possi-bilities, fun and camaraderie, and basking in nature.

Through free writing, I came up with my paradigm: "Everything is a lesson for living with more freedom." It's changed from time to time, but the freedom bit is a constant.

It's my experience with clients who do this exercise that they experience a sense of clarity about their relationship with golf, and what's important to them about the game.

In doing this exercise, it's not unusual for people to have a significant reaction such as, "Wow. This is why I play golf." Some discover—and quite often, rediscover—that their why is connected to their passions, aspirations, and what they are searching or striving for, not just in their golf, but in their life.

People who do this exercise generally come up with one major why, and some generate a number of them. Don't judge your why. It doesn't need to be lofty or ambitious, just that it has meaning for you. Your why might be about becoming a single-digit golfer who has fun. Or being resilient in tournaments and tough situations. Or letting go and having goofy fun with friends. Or developing psychologically or spiritually.

This exercise reveals many things that are less obvious than our ego-driven cravings. Most of what we write during this process moves us from the negative to the positive and represents ways of being that we are striving for, and our vision of our best self.

When we write our aspirations down, we are taking action to bring them closer to fruition. Rather than just "thinking about" actions we might take, writing them down makes them more substantial, and we move closer to taking actions that fulfil the commitments we make to ourselves. Just the act of writing is taking action.

Writing why you play golf brings your core values and goals into greater consciousness so you can use them as guidance to create the future you've chosen for yourself.

Staying on your chosen path moves you forward. When you are focused on your mission, the improvements you're seeking will start showing up in your ball-striking, your self-management, your decision-making, and scoring. No doubt your improvements will show up slower than you'd like, but they will. You will find that you are less compulsive and not as bothered by the inevitable slumps, bad breaks, and mysterious afflictions that every golfer suffers.

You'll continue to struggle with golf because it's a hard game, but you may not be a crestfallen or panicked as you were before. As the writer Anne Lamott has said about trying to make progress in our lives, it's "scooch, scooch, stall, scooch, stall, catastrophic reversal, bog, bog, scooch."

That's golf and life.

THE ACTION YOU CAN TAKE TO GET UNSTUCK

The Why Do I Play Golf exercise provides you with the foundation for developing your mission.

After doing this exercise, re-visit the Second Practice chapter and begin to draft your mission or paradigm. As with any writing, allow yourself to write freely; just let the words flow on to the page without editing. The draft stage of any writing process is like dumping your brains on the page, which means it will likely be messy, incomplete, jumbled, incoherent and disorganized, among other things. That's great. The goal is to get whatever is in your head on the page.

As you did with this exercise, just let it be for a few hours or a day. Then re-read it and start to make any changes you believe will sharpen and clarify it. The revision process also takes time, so be patient. As you revise, you'll start to shorten it to its essential elements. It often takes several revisions over the course of days, weeks or even months to arrive at something that resonates and feels like your truth.

Once you're happy with it, I suggest that you write out your mission or paradigm and keep it where you can see it often, such as near your bathroom mirror or in your office. Write it on your scorecard or in your yardage book. You might even print it and laminate it and keep it in your golf bag.

Note that your mission or paradigm may change over time, which is fine. If you feel it doesn't seem to ring true, you might revisit your "Why" or even take another run at it, and then go through the draft-revision process again. This is a practice you can do for the rest of your life.

With your mission in place, you might find that a blow-up hole or a high score doesn't sting as much because you know that's not ultimately what's most important to you. You might even find that you feel lighter, more relaxed, and you enjoy the beautiful surroundings or your playing partners more. And that you are creating new behaviours that serve you.

HERE ARE SOME "WHY'S" FROM SOME FRIENDS AND CLIENTS:

- *I started golf because of work. I was among a few women to play at the time. My brother was a scratch golfer, and he emphasized that I should always have fun, and don't take it too seriously. I was hooked once I figured out how to hit that little white ball. I'm an A-type. I had to learn patience and mental endurance. I learned quickly that getting frustrated wasn't who I was, and frankly it doesn't help the game. So, I focus on enjoying the experience, nature, and the company and, of course, a good walk.*

- *I play golf because I enjoy it. But at times I let the frustrations of the game cloud the enjoyment. So, the goal this year is to leave every round with a positive attitude and feeling. A big part of enjoying golf is playing with people I enjoy being with. Part of feeling positive about golf for me is putting in the work to get better and seeing the results.*

- *I play golf for peace and quiet. I am a huge talker but not on the golf course. I love the silence of the course. My favourite sound is the ball dropping in the cup. I never take a gimmie for that reason. I love to go home and talk about my game with anyone who will listen.*

- *My objectives for the season in order of importance are exercise, be distracted from the pressures of life, the need to compete, being outside, being with friends, and play business golf with customers. My core objectives: qualify for senior provincial championships and win the Senior Club Championship at my club. In the end, these tie into "why I play" as a sense of accomplishment and being able to do so proficiently. But I can't tell you how many times I've played by myself and just enjoyed the moment regardless of my score. These are Zen-type moments that tie into the meaning of life to me!*

- *I love the challenge of tournament golf. There is a Golf Channel in my head where I am the star. I've worked hard, I'm prepared and raring to go. I have specific goals for sure— GIR improvement, nailing down the 100-yard-and-in game, and maintaining some distance gains off the tee. It's all part of the plan but is not the plan. I would love to hold a trophy at some point, but in the end, my goal is to keep it a positive experience that enhances my life and the lives of my family and friends.*

- *My key objective this year is to be injury-free!! Ever since I had my hip replaced six years ago, some physical injury seems to hinder my game each year. So, I have been working harder than usual on improving my upper body strength, which I hope will help me get back to a 14-handicap. I play because it's great physical exercise (if you walk!). I also love being outside, enjoying the fresh air and communing with nature.*

- *My core objectives this golf season are to get to a 2.0 handicap, achieve 160-mph ball speed, and be on our club's Ryder Cup team. Why Do I Play Golf: Like other members, my club is like home. I love putting on my headphones early in the morning and hitting balls, chipping, pitching, and putting. I'm there to experience the sweetness of a pure strike, the smell of the cut grass, the sun rising and gradually warming up the air. I love all the challenges golf asks of me.*

- *My objectives for this season are to continue to test my ability to perform better under pressure situations. This may seem like a simple notion, but it encompasses all the reasons why I play golf. I love the challenge of managing my state on and off the golf course. A big part of my raison d'etre is to test my awareness skills, and whether I can be present in any golf situation. The process fascinates me.*

Things to do to get unstuck

- Get a notebook or just three pieces of paper, write Why Do I Play Golf across the top, and start writing.
- Don't stop until you're finished all three pages.
- What's the most important part? Writing it.

A golf intervention

In the summer of 2019, I was pulling my drives left—auto-reload-instant-double-bogey-left-of-left left.

Exasperated, I reached out to George McNamara, whom I met at an Extraordinary Golf coaches' workshop delivered by Fred Shoemaker two years earlier. We connected and became friends. George had been a PGA of America Master Professional for nearly 25 years and operated The Golf Zone golf and entertainment facility in Honey Brook, Pennsylvania. He was also a friend of Fred's.

I sent George some videos. He noted that my head was well behind the ball in my set up. I needed to get my head more over the ball to move my weight more forward. My driving improved instantly. I still hit the occasional drive left, but only periodically. I was ecstatic.

However, as the weeks went on, the magic began to wane. I reached way back into my bag of swing thoughts and found an old nugget where I focused keeping my lead foot firmly planted on the ground both back and through. Eureka! It worked! I was killing it. Oh joy, oh bliss.

I excitedly went into the next round. I hit four drives dead left in eight holes, leading to a front-nine 46. The score didn't bother me that much. It was my reaction.

I confessed my shame in an email to George:

"What concerned me the most was that I played holes 5-11 in a state of barely contained rage. I could not let my anger go. Everything I teach my clients went out the window.

"I was a petulant, pouting, fast-walking, no-talking angry man. I was *that* guy. I thought: 'I fucking hate this. When am I ever going to get this game? When will I finally take my game to the next level?'

"I left the course angry, drove home like a mad little boy, banged cupboards at home and put on the loudest, angriest music I could find." (If you must know, it was *Break Stuff* by Limp Bizkit. Don't play it with kids in earshot.)

I shared the email with Howard Glassman, co-host of our *Swing Thoughts* podcast. He suggested we invite George on the podcast for an "intervention."[1]

George reminded me that changing parts of a golf motion takes a long time. He said: "If you are just looking at outcomes, nothing is going to change. Outcomes are always changing. If you are looking for a process to change the outcome, that's where learning takes place."

I exclaimed: "George! I know!"

I said that my swing wasn't the issue. I knew about the power of process and all that. I was distraught by my bratty behaviour.

---

[1] Check out episode #107. Fast forward to the 26th minute for our discussion with George. It's pretty funny.

It was contrary to everything I learned as a caddie, and the cool, calm, and occasionally amusing demeanour that I attempted to project out to the world no matter what noxious poisons were roiling around inside my head. It contradicted my carefully contrived image that I was "a nice golfer to play with" because I was always encouraging and even picked up other people's garbage and fixed their ball marks.

I was angry and mystified that I had been yanked right back into my old stuff like an addict. I fell back into a pattern of alleviating my anxiety by grasping onto anything that I felt might instantly solve the problem.

My knee-jerk reaction had nothing to do with logic and being a grounded person worthy of your admiration. It was compulsion. I felt out of control, desperate. I wanted out of my misery. In seeking salvation, I was like an alcoholic under stress reaching for a drink.

George said I had a choice: I could certainly play golf focused on results. Or I could play golf so I could take something positive out of every round. It sounded so mature, extraordinarily wise, and devoted, like a monk getting up at 2 a.m. to chant.

George suggested that I play the "awareness game."

"You can ask yourself on the first tee, 'What's my intention? What do I want to pay attention to for the next four hours?' So that whether you hit it left or right, you're evaluating if you stayed focused on your intention, not on the result. In an awareness game, you cannot lose."

Like all good coaches, George knew what he was talking about because he had lived it. He related his own experience with learning the value of intention and having a mission.

George said that while he was attending his first Extraordinary Golf coaches' workshop, he told Fred Shoemaker that he was frustrated that he wasn't making faster progress. Fred laid one of his Fred-isms on George: "When your commitment to your intention is greater than your addiction to an outcome, you'll change your golf swing."

George asked, "Are you calling me an addict?"

Fred: "Yes."

George: "Whoa!"

In relating the story to Howard and I, George said, "Fred hit me right between the eyes."

Sadly, George died in 2022 at the age of 73 after a battle with cancer.

Coaching Yourself Through Journaling

For a golf nerd, the famous adage nails it: "Golf is not a matter of life and death. It's more important than that."

We greatly anticipate most every round. We bring a lot more than our clubs and balls to the first tee: we also bring our expectations, hopes and whatever swing thought we're counting on that day to connect us with the sweet spot.

When golf means this much to you, every round can feel like you're trudging through deep valleys and slogging up steep hills shrouded in inky blackness with rare glimpses of sunlight. The monsters that were under your bed when you were a kid are now behind trees and hiding in bunkers. You can't see the gremlins, but you can hear them.

After the round, we review what went well and didn't. Despite the islets of joy we may experience, most of us dwell on the negative. With the harshness of a critic with an axe to grind, we sharply criticize and judge ourselves. This makes us think of things that we hope will fix our problems and make us feel better.

We engage in behaviours that are largely fueled by our anxieties, compulsions, and cravings, which keep us stuck in Stuckville.

How do we avoid this cyclical pattern? By developing perspective and acknowledging that our expectations are not serving us.

Here's some perspective: Fred Shoemaker says most golfers mishit 50-80 per cent of their shots, they score well only once out of every four rounds, and even for their lowest rounds, they would be happier if they shot five shots lower. "Welcome to golf," Fred says. "To play this game, you must have an extraordinary relationship with failure."

What if you could develop the perspective that golf—and failure—provide you with an opportunity to learn something from your experience?

This leads us to another practice that you, the golf nerd, can use to increase your awareness and become free of old patterns.

This leads us to journaling. All your need is a pen and a notebook. If you want a fancy leather-bound tome, go for it. But a spiral notebook like your kid in Grade 9 uses is just fine.

To borrow a phrase from the therapy world, your journal holds space for you. It is the place where you can share anything confidentially. Of course, it's completely up to you how deep you want to go with it.

To paraphrase George Carlin, most men—and it appears to me that a growing number of women—would rather touch flaming wood than share their feelings and vulnerable thoughts with anyone. It's a damn shame. It allows you to work through your stuff. And feels good when you disgorge the toxins from your gut.

Golf nerds are harsh critics prone to berating themselves

mercilessly and keeping a meticulous inventory of their deficiencies and screw-ups. Like the beliefs and stories we developed as children about ourselves, we carry memories and feelings from our rounds forward, and they have a powerful effect on us.

Our memories become our foundation for our golf, and how we explain ourselves to ourselves:

- Of course, I choked. I'm a choker!
- I always hit it in the water on No. 8.
- Whenever I have a good round going, I screw it up.
- I can't get off the first tee when there's a crowd watching.
- I suck at bunkers. Always have, always will.
- Coach was right. I'm not athletic.

Memory is exceedingly powerful. In their book, *Be a Player*, Pia Nilsson and Lynn Marriott explain: "(Memory) is a central construct of our identities. Memory is the physio-neural mechanism by which we encode, store, and recall information important to our lives. Memory gives us the capability to access previous experiences, as well as to adapt to new ones …. When we experience something, it gets imprinted and internally represented in specific areas of our brain."

Given the importance of memory and its impact on our golf and our lives, the practice of journaling is essential. Journaling is like a lifeline that keeps you afloat, helps you work through problems, vent your emotions, maintain perspective, document significant insights and experiences, explore your thoughts, maintain a record like a database, express gratitude, feel more at peace … and that's just getting started.

Even if you don't write often and lack confidence in your writing, I believe it's crucial that all golf nerds keep some kind of journal. (If calling it a notebook makes it more palatable for you, go for it.) Journaling allows you to express those thoughts that you aren't willing to share out loud with your buddies; your journal is a safe space to vent, rage, and release the crap that spins around your head.

If you try journaling, you will be surprised at how your thoughts and feelings diminish—all without needing alcohol, gummies, or another numbing distraction. You can also celebrate and anchor the good stuff that you might not proclaim on the clubhouse patio. Journaling provides an opportunity to process what you experienced on the course and how it affected you.

As Karl Morris has said, golf has three distinct periods: before golf, during golf, and after golf. Morris says that most golfers tend to ignore or downplay the importance of our post-round thoughts to our peril. This is when most golfers make decisions that affect future rounds. If you don't find your equilibrium after a round, you'll remain agitated and off balance mentally. This keeps you in your habit loop, cycling through the triggers, thoughts and behaviours that keep you stuck.

Your patterns of thinking and behaving have the greatest influence on the quality of your golf. Most golfers think it's their swing mechanics. Ultimately, anyone who plays the game skillfully has sound fundamentals. But if you panic practice, chronically seek advice or instructional content, you'll be in a constant state of intellectualizing, self-criticism, confusion, and desperation. You will not develop skill deliberately and progressively.

HOW JOURNALING HELPS YOU LEARN FROM EVERY ROUND

Here are some thoughts on how to journal and why the practice can assist you in learning from every round you play, keep you focused on your mission or paradigm, and increase your ability to be aware of what you're thinking and doing.

A. Get a notebook or journal that you will enjoy writing in, and it has enough pages to contain a season's worth of entries. Use a pen that flows freely that allows you to write quickly. As I noted in the section on Why Do I Play Golf, if you prefer to use a computer, that's OK. Some people are more auditory and enjoy dictating into their phone. Use whatever medium makes it easy to record and review your entries.

B. After every round, dedicate yourself to write about it. But you don't need to write an epic. Commit to filling *one page* in your journal.[1]

The commitment to fill a certain amount of space is important because it's easy to give up on the days when the words aren't coming easily, or you'd just rather stop thinking about your round. When you feel lousy, it's natural that you want to escape by distracting yourself or numbing your feelings. (It's no mystery to me that alcohol is the preferred drug of choice among golfers; it's society's approved way to escape bad feelings.)

As with all the writing exercises in this book, let the pen go. Don't edit, judge, look out the window to ponder your deepest truths, cross words out you think are stupid, look things up on

---

[1] If you feel like writing more, go for it. Let whatever is in your head pour out.

the internet, or wash the dishes while you wait for inspiration. Keep the pen moving and allow the words to spill on to the page. My mother called it the "hot pen method." You can't do this wrong. (It's like meditation.) No one will see it except you.

This is called free writing. When you free write, you drop under your self-conscious and controlling ego mind and get into the muck and mire—as well as the sweetness and light—of your subconscious. You can tap into your feelings, values, dreams, and your essence. Your true self.

Just like hitting a golf shot, many people tend to self-interfere when they write because they are self-conscious about doing it right. When we're judging, comparing, and thinking about what we're doing, we can't access our talent, skill, and experience— as a golfer, writer, businessperson, or in anything.

Free writing allows you to work through whatever you are feeling and thinking. You may find that you end up doing a process known as RAIN on the page. That is, you'll be recognizing what's happening, accepting it (by writing about it), investigating it, and ultimately detaching your identity from your feelings and stories. In this place, you can also have compassion for yourself.

RAIN is a mindfulness process popularized by Tara Brach, a prominent podcaster and therapist who brings a Buddhist perspective to her approach. RAIN is an acronym for the key elements of the practice:

> *R—Recognize what is happening*
> *A—Allow it*
> *I—Investigate with kindness*
> *N—Non-Identification and Nourish*

__Recognize__ that you're caught up in something. The first step is to simply be aware of what's happening in your head and your body. (Your body is the gateway to feelings.)

__Allow__ whatever is happening to, well, happen. There's no need to stop it or make it go away (through alcohol, busyness, TV, etc.). You cannot move forward or heal if you are unaware of what's going on. So let it be. Sometimes that's all you need—by recognizing and allowing—to return to feeling more peaceful and in the moment.

__Investigate what's happening.__ Ask yourself, "What's happening inside me?" You might also ask "What am I believing?" "When have I felt this before?" Brach says to treat yourself as if your child came home in tears after being bullied. That is, investigate with kindness.

__Non-identification.__ This means you don't identify with the stories, beliefs, and judgments swirling around your head. You observe them but you do not define yourself by these messages—they're just the stories we make up about ourselves based on our past.

N also stands for __nourish__. When you are suffering, __nourish__ yourself—offer yourself some kindness. Your journal is your private, safe space.

This may strike some readers as soft and contrary to their belief that you should never let yourself off the hook. I'm not saying you shouldn't hold yourself accountable or hold yourself to the highest standard. I'm saying that rather than shame and judge yourself, that you witness yourself as a person who is worthy of respect, who owns their mistakes and self-defeating behaviours, and is committed to taking on actions toward a new way of being their best self.

Expressing your feelings and thoughts on the page is like talking about them; it feels good, you distance yourself from them, and the intensity of your feelings tends to diminish. The objective is not to make your feelings *go away*, but to find your way back to clarity and emotional neutrality *through* them. Resistance perpetuates your suffering; abiding in and allowing is a pathway to resolution. (There's wisdom in the maxim, "What we resist persists.")

When you read your journal, you may notice that you become like the witness; that is, you observe your mind in a more detached manner. In fact, you can practice observing yourself as a separate entity. When we witness what's happening within us, we can detach from the grip of our feelings and stories. We see our behaviours more clearly. It's as if we're seeing them happen in someone else.

This is another example of how awareness is curative.

Awareness is vitally important in getting unstuck and transforming because the habits of our personality let go most completely when we see them as they are happening.[2]

We tend to write in a logical progression. Rather than just having thoughts pinging around in your brain as they usually do, one thought after another, writing allows you to record your thoughts in an orderly way which makes it easier to make sense of them.

As you read and reflect on what you've written, you'll naturally evaluate and consider it. (This is where your compulsion

[2]Don Richard Riso and Russ Hudson. The Wisdom of the Enneagram. Bantam, page 90.

to judge can serve you.) You will often see that things aren't as bad or bleak as you first thought, or you realize that you're caught once again in a story or belief. As per the N in the RAIN acronym—non-identification—you will develop awareness that you don't need to identify with your stories and beliefs.

As you write in your journal, you may find that you begin encouraging and affirming yourself. This may sound squishy for some readers, but having compassion for yourself leads to greater understanding, clarity, and keeps you sailing on your chosen path.

From a place of conscious awareness, you can discern more clearly from the circumstances of each round, learn more about yourself, and determine the concrete actions that you will take to serve you. Journaling allows you to express, process and even plan on how—as a golf nerd—you choose to fulfil your personal vision.

I believe we all want to feel connected to something larger and more powerful than ourselves. We are striving for both a sense of personal fulfilment and connection.

Regardless of your belief system, I think you can take something powerful from Richard Rohr: "The deepest human need and longing is to overcome the separateness, the distance from what always seems over there, and beyond me, like a perfect lover, a moment of perfection in art, music or dance, and surely a transcendent God."

Things to do to get unstuck

- Get a journal or a notebook.
- After every round, write at least one page about your experience.

- Re-read it later and note some of the key points about what you learned, and you can take forward into your next practice and game.

- As you ponder possible actions you're going to take, consider them in context of your mission or paradigm.

My eureka moment with Dr. Jud

In the world of broadcasting and podcasting, there are people known as "great gets." It's not unlike the feeling that you somehow ended up with someone who is "out of your league."

One of those great gets on our *Swing Thoughts* podcast was Dr. Judson Brewer, a psychiatrist at Yale University who has become well-known through his *TedTalks* and books such as *The Craving Mind* which integrate mindfulness with psychology. I first became aware of Brewer in 2017 while driving on the busy Highway 401 west of Toronto. I was listening to *10% Happier*, a podcast by Dan Harris.[1]

On this episode, Brewer was talking about addiction, focusing on the usual suspects—cigarettes, alcohol, overeating, and smartphones. Brewer defined addiction as any behaviour that

---

[1]Brewer has been a guest many times on *10% Happier*, which focuses on meditation and related subjects such as Buddhism and psychology. This appearance was episode #61.

we repeat even though we know it's harmful. "Continued use despite adverse consequences," he added.

He explained that, like everything in our lives, the factors that lead to addiction begin in the brain. As humans evolved, our brains helped us survive by remembering where we found food by releasing dopamine, which we regard today as the feel-good hormone. Brewer said our brains still work this way.

What does a dopamine hit feel like? Think about when you sink your teeth into a gooey chocolate cupcake, take that first sip of coffee in the morning, or a putt drops in the hole.[2] It feels good! The spritz of dopamine is the reward for the behaviour.

Eventually, we also learn that a dopamine hit can also dull pain, such was when we're feeling bad, stressed or even bored. So, we'll eat the cupcake even though we're not hungry, take a drink to relax, or check our smartphone for texts or likes. The dopamine hit dulls our pain momentarily. This is how we create a cycle that perpetuates itself and reinforces what's known as a habit loop (aka addiction).

You may wonder what this has to do with golf. Stay with me. I believe this explains a lot about behaviours that keep golf nerds stuck.

Brewer said there are three key elements of the habit loop: trigger, behaviour, and reward.

For a smoker, the loop could start with: he gets a coffee (trigger), lights a cigarette (behaviour), and inhales the smoke and gets a nicotine hit (reward). For an alcoholic, the loop could start

---

[2]Yes, you certainly get a dopamine hit when you have an orgasm.

with: she has an argument with her partner (trigger), she opens a bottle of wine (behaviour), and drinks it and gets an alcoholic buzz (reward).

After Brewer explained the habit loop to Harris, it hit me. "Oh my God! This is what I do with golf." I was gobsmacked. I distinctly remember looking at myself in the rearview mirror; I was beaming. I wanted to bookmark the moment. Talk about a dopamine hit! Of course, I needed to know more.

I invited Brewer on to our podcast.[3] Howard and I peppered him with questions about the habit loop and addiction—Howard is a reformed smoker and he's been sober since 2015—and I excitedly told Dr. Jud how I thought the trigger-behaviour-reward habit loop applied to my golf.

Trigger—I am struggling with my game. I feel compelled to do something to fix a problem. I obsess, think about, and seek solutions.

Behaviour—I go to the range and pound balls.

Reward—I eventually find something that "works," usually a swing thought like "turn my left hip." I feel happy, emboldened, and excited that my next round will confirm I've ascended to the next level.

But as sure as the sun rises every day, the magic of whatever worked no longer does. By the fifth hole, I'm a million over par, disappointed yet again and frustrated. Then I cycle through my habit loop for the kajillionth time.

I asked Dr. Jud if my experience exemplified the habit loop.

---

[3] To listen to this conversation, check out episode #41 of *Swing Thoughts*. Dr. Jud was a great guest, and we had a lot of fun.

"Ding, ding, ding," he said, laughing.

He explained that it wasn't bad technique that was causing me to feel stuck in a habit loop of self-destructive behaviours. It was my craving and my addictive patterns. I was like an addict seeking the dopamine hit to feel better.

He added: "You're looking for love in all the wrong places."

He said I was looking extrinsically (outside of myself) for my reward—to feel good— rather than looking intrinsically (inside).

"If we're looking outside of ourselves to try to fix something that's not broken in the first place, we're going to constantly be looking for a new technique," he said. "If you're going out to shoot a certain score, that's an 'in order to.' It's based on an extrinsic reward.

"If the trigger is the thought to shoot a certain score, and we're on our way to shoot that score, and we do it, we feel good. Then we set this expectation—external reward—I'm going to do that again.

"But when we're on track to not do that, it's the death spiral," he said. "We start to get worried and in our own way. That extrinsic motivator is a ticking time bomb."

I listened over and over to this episode, and then one day Brewer's metaphor hit me: I cruise along, sometime for years, trying to hold my anger down—until I'm so stressed that I can't keep it down anymore.

Boom!

This was a new piece of the puzzle in understanding my behaviour, and why I was forever revisiting old swing thoughts, trying out new ones, and failing to stay true to my commitments. And suffering the occasional nuclear meltdown.

His explanation of how our behaviours keep us stuck also aligned with my reading, my experience in the ManKind Project, and the experiences of many of my golf and life coaching clients. That is, despite our desires to be better golfers, partners, parents, and workers, and the actions that we take to change, most of us repeat the same self-destructive behaviours over and over.

Continued use despite adverse consequences.

My experience with Judson Brewer was one of many that caused me to start looking in a different place—at my intrinsic motivators, such as trusting myself, staying true to my commitments, having fun, connecting with my partners, and feeling gratitude.

The irony, of course, is that by pursuing the intrinsic reward, I also get the reward of shooting better scores. In my mid-60s, I started to play the best golf of my life.

Quite obviously, as my intervention and 2023 club championship proved, I'm still messy, the product of seven decades of thinking, feeling, and behaving. That's why I use the practices in this book—to increase my self-awareness. It's a slow process, like I'm peeling another layer of an onion that has an infinite number of layers.

That's the work. Taking full responsibility for your actions, acknowledging where you're out of integrity with yourself and others, learning more about yourself, and committing to the actions that create your new future. There are no guarantees. But these practices will move you forward, perhaps in ways that you didn't foresee, and reveal gifts and opportunities that you didn't know you had.

Things to do to get unstuck

You can learn more about the habit loop, and specifically about *your* habit loops, by visiting www.drjud.com and navigate to "Unwinding-Anxiety-Habit-Mapper-from-DrJud."

The "habit mapper" is free, and an excellent way to learn more about the triggers, behaviours, and rewards that you routinely engage in that keep you stuck. Increasing your awareness inches you closer to getting unstuck and moving forward.

Anchoring Your Best Experiences

*"If it wasn't for bad luck,
I wouldn't have no luck at all."*

Born Under a Bad Sign
Performed by Albert King and Cream
Written by William Bell and Booker T. Jones

When I became an assistant coach of the University of Guelph golf team, I quickly recognized a behaviour that I'd witnessed many times on clubhouse patios and in grillrooms.

On the bus rides back to campus from tournaments, the players, especially the guys, would quickly wallow in a whine-fest about all their gruesome lip-outs, horrific lies, et al.

They'd tell these stories with relish, regaling each other with tales of bad luck and trouble worthy of a lugubrious blues dirge, while also playing a game of one-upmanship. One player would finish his story and the next would say, "Oh, you think that was bad ...."

Like guys do, they'd tell these stories for laughs, and the odd sense of connection they get in telling them. It's a cool trick. They are being vulnerable with each other in a way that's acceptable. Rather being the hero or the broken-hearted sap, they play the role of the Joker, who holds himself up for ridicule while others envy his ability to hold court and make everyone laugh.

It's certainly healthy to laugh at ourselves. When you four-putt or find your ball in a deep divot angled away from the green, you're not laughing. Maybe later, but the story is rooted in pain, or at least resigned ambivalence born of previous calamities. It's a reminder of this equation: Pain + Time = Comedy.

As I discussed in the chapter on journaling, when you dwell on your golf tragedies rather than on the good stuff, you are unwittingly setting yourself up for future misery. When you invest energy in your stories—no matter how tragicomic they are—you are anchoring them in your memories. When you face similar situations in the future, you are prone to feeling a sense of danger or dread that something bad is about to happen.

Our minds recall events in which we felt extremes of emotion to protect us from future pain. Karl Morris provides an interesting nugget about the role of memory and emotion. He says that if you try to remember a random birthday from, say, 15 years ago, you likely won't remember it. But if it was a major celebration with friends and family of a milestone birthday from, say, turning 40 or 50, you are far more likely to remember it because of the emotions you felt. Memories encoded in strong feelings will replay themselves whether we want to remember them or not.

Having experienced this phenomenon, when I became head coach of the university golf team, I instituted a practice for the team.

At the end of every tournament, each player would answer the following three questions in order:

1. What are you feeling?
2. Describe your best shot of the day with as much detail as possible.
3. What did you learn today that you can take forward into practice and your next round?

This allowed the players to invest their energy and emotions in a positive moment that they could call upon later. (I encouraged them to record them in their journals as well.)

When you have handled situations well and had experiences that you feel good about, you're more likely to perform well when you encounter similar situations in the future. This is generally what people mean when they say they feel confident.

It's just common sense: you'll feel more relaxed, more secure, and decisive. It doesn't mean you'll hit the ball perfectly, but you will be more likely to perform well. I once asked Fred Couples what he thought about when he faced a shot under pressure. He said that he'd often think of the best shot he ever hit with that club and then hit his shot. I admire Fred Couples for being so direct, succinct, and sharp.

This is the background to my recommendation for The Fifth Practice:

Record your three best shots of the round.

However, rather than focus on the *results* of those shots, it's far more valuable to focus on the experience you had. It's totally cool to write about shots that got the results you intended, such as making a long birdie putt or you spun a wedge to tap-in, but that tends to play to your ego.

It's more valuable to record the three experiences that you'd like to anchor, learn from, and remember (like Fred Couples). The suggestion is that you write about experiences in which you, for example:

- Learned something about hitting a particular kind of shot.
- Had a valuable insight.
- Stayed true to your commitment or intention.
- Followed your process.
- Enjoyed the feeling and thoughts you had in deciding upon a shot.
- Backed off a shot and re-committed.
- Assessed a difficult situation well.
- Became aware of negative thinking and became more present.
- Felt something in your swing that you'd like to feel again.
- You envisioned your ball flight and just let the shot go.

These are just suggestions. Write about whatever you like, but the objective is to record experiences that provide you with greater insight into yourself, expand your awareness, increase your learning, and allow you to anchor processes or patterns that have value for you. Write as much detail as you can.

For example, let's say there's a hole on your course that gives you fits, and you've been working on committing to good targets. During your pre-shot process, you found yourself thinking about the pond left of the green, but you committed to hitting a draw to the right side of the green. You picked a tree behind the green as your target. Let's say the ball finished on the green 15 feet right of the flag.

Nice! The value of the experience, however, is not the result. The value is that you executed your intention to commit to a target.

The beauty of recording your three best shots is that the practice increases your ability to tap into valuable learning experiences in the future. A result is ephemeral. Here and gone. As Fred Shoemaker has said, today's results are no predictors of tomorrow's success. But you can take learning forward and it has an enormous influence on future performance.

It's up to you when you write about your three best experiences from a round, but recording them on the same day allows you to recall the fine details. You can record them as part of your journaling practice.

Or you can write them just before you go to bed. This is an opportune time because what we're focused on just before we fall asleep tends to be replayed in our subconscious as we sleep. Besides, drifting off with the memory of good things playing in your head just seems like a nice way to end the day.

Our inner wisdom resides in our subconscious. It's the repository for our gold—our values, greatest attributes, talents, and the best parts of our selves. When you're playing your best golf and being your best self, you are accessing that gold. When you are recording your best experiences, I strongly believe you're investing in yourself and your gold grows.

Things to do to get unstuck

- Record your three best shots of the day.
- Read your entries with any eye for how they align with your why, and your mission.
- Consider experiences and anchors that you can draw upon during your next practice or round.
- Periodically review several of your entries and note the dominant themes; this helps anchor these experiences so you can draw on them on the course.

A punk reminder on how you get good at golf

One of the greatest things about playing in a punk band is just telling people, "I play bass in a punk band."[1]

I love the surprised look on people's faces that a man in his 60s who plays and coaches golf plays in a punk band. "Gee, you don't have any tattoos." The northward advance of my forehead has also precluded a mohawk.

What does this have to do with getting good at golf?

The connection I'm making is that learning to play a song flawlessly as an individual or with a group neatly parallels the process of developing your golf game. Or mastering anything that involves performance. The challenge is to work your way intelligently and patiently through the learning process to the point that you completely own what you're doing.

---

[1] If you consider punk chaotic noise, you haven't listened to the The Clash album *London Calling*. Great punk music has a rawness that gives it a delicious edge, but it is remarkably precise.

Each summer while university is adjourned, our band C.I.D is joined for a few months by Michaela Watkins, our lead guitarist's niece. She adds sweet flavouring to our all-male band with great harmonies, but she can also confidently belt out lead vocals.

To showcase Michaela, we play three or four songs expressly for her to sing. As we prepared for a big fundraising event one summer, we thought that *Only Happy When It Rains*, a powerful and emotive song by Garbage, would be perfect. We rehearsed it over the course of two practices leading to the event.

At the show, we cruised through half-a-dozen songs—most of which we've been playing for three to five years—and launched into *Only Happy When It Rains*. We got through the first verse and chorus, but then everyone got lost. We looked wide-eyed at each other wondering how we were going to rescue this disaster when Michaela raised her fist over her head—the agreed-upon signal for the ending—and brought it down. Our nightmare was mercifully over.

We all agreed that we performed the song before we owned it. Our intentions were good, but it was a mistake to try it. We got caught up in the excitement of debuting a new song. We could play the song competently in practice—a band's version of a driving range—but it wasn't ready for prime time.

It's the same thing when learning a new—or old—move in your golf swing. On the range, you may think you've mastered a move, and go into your next game thinking you're one step from the tour. But on the course, the magic is AWOL. Poof. Gone. This happens over and over.

Here's the part that no one wants to read:

Whenever you hear or see anyone performing at a high level, that person has invested a massive amount of time and quality practice to get there. "There is an irrefutable law of living that everyone understands yet so many fight against … if you want to get good at something you have to do it a lot," personal trainer Paul Landini wrote in *The Globe and Mail*.

This is the basis for the oft-misunderstood 10,000-hour rule popularized by Malcolm Gladwell in his book *Outliers*, which misled many people to think that anyone who spends a significant amount of time doing anything will somehow become world-class.

To master a skill requires 10,000 hours of deliberate practice that includes *targeted, mistake-focused practice*, said researcher Anders Ericsson. "You need to be practicing with purpose," Ericsson told the BBC.[2]

This runs counter to the culture of golf which proclaims that if you digest the right information and apply it, you'll get the result you want. As Fred Shoemaker has said, golfers think that if they do Y, they will get X. It's not true. This also runs counter to the way the majority of golfers behave: rather than focusing on a few key elements until they have mastered them, they flit from tip to tip, buying this training device, or that speed trainer, and trying to adapt to the latest theory or method.[3]

---

[2] BBC: How to master new skills with deliberate practice. https://www.bbc.com/worklife/article/20190318-how-to-master-new-skills-with-deliberate-practice.

[3] I recall my father trying to master the Square-to-Square method when I was around 15, which only caused him to keep the clubface disastrously closed through the swing. Many other methods have come

Most golfers rarely master anything before flying off to try something new. The problem is not that they are incapable of learning; rather they feel compelled to constantly search for fixes and secrets they hope will solve their problems and make them happy.

This chronic swing-fixing doesn't allow for learning that leads to high performance. It doesn't provide enough time for your brain to change in a positive way. According to Daniel Coyle, author of *The Talent Code*, mastering a move in your golf swing results from "precisely timed electrical signals traveling through a chain of neurons—a circuit of nerve fibres. (A substance called) myelin forms around these circuits as a kind of insulation that increases signal strength, speed, and accuracy. The more we fire a particular circuit, the more myelin optimizes that circuit, and the stronger, faster, and more fluent our movements become."

This explains why the best golfers you know are remarkably consistent, such as the senior club champ who has kept his index low for decades, or the twenty-something with the swing to die for. At some stage, they went through an intensive learning stage until they owned their swings.

Our band didn't take the time to practice that song until we owned it. I find so many parallels between golf and performance of any kind because developing your golf game

and gone, including Hogan's Secret, Stack and Tilt, The X-Factor, The A-Swing, and more. A few years ago, the secret to better golf was "shallowing out your swing." I don't hear that much anymore. Did it stop working?

encompasses creativity, learning, and performance skills.[4]

Like golfers who are constantly trying to follow tips they've learned online, music producer Rick Rubin says artists who copy trendy sounds produce terrible music. Rubin has produced Run DMC, Red Hot Chili Peppers, AC/DC, Tom Petty, Sheryl Crow, Johnny Cash, Ed Sheeran, Lady Gaga, and more.

When you are impatient and try to force a certain result, you interrupt the creative process. "Impatience is an argument with reality," Rubin writes in his book, *The Creative Act.*

Here's where I think Rubin absolutely nails it, especially for golfers: "Time is something you have no control over. So, patience begins with acceptance of natural rhythms. The implied benefit of impatience is to save time by speeding up and skipping ahead of those rhythms. The desire for something to be different from what we are experiencing in the here and now ....

"Paradoxically, this ends up taking more time and using more energy. It's wasted effort ... Patience is required for the nuanced development of your craft."

Fred Shoemaker says that golfers seeking to change their swings must be patient. In an email, Shoemaker said that during the early stages of the learning process, the most important thing is to dramatically slow down your motion. When you swing too fast, it's impossible to be aware of what you are doing.[5]

---

[4]Howard and I have had many discussions on the podcast about how playing golf—especially tournament golf—is like one of the scariest and toughest things: standing on a stage and trying to make people laugh. It requires preparation, presence, awareness, and certainly experience.

[5]As an example of patience, Shoemaker spent nine months on changing his swing plane by a few inches.

When he's working on his swing, Shoemaker says he'll swing at 20 per cent of his regular speed and monitor his swing on video. When the video shows that he's making solid progress, he'll make swings at 40 per cent speed. Only when he can repeat a move correctly—as seen on video—does he hit a ball, but only at about 50 per cent speed.

"If I go faster than my awareness, I'll probably grab power from old, familiar, and ineffective sources, my sequencing will be off, and my swing will look as it's always looked," he wrote. "My body must learn this new sequencing from this new place. This takes patience!"

To develop skill that elevates your ball-striking and improves your scoring requires commitment to a process, or as I mentioned, a mission. When you commit to a mission, the results will come.

A commitment could be one of the following:

- Working with a coach.
- Developing a practice plan that you stick to.
- Having one practice session a week devoted to your short game.
- Devoting your season to learning how to hit shots that fly on a certain trajectory, or eliminating the fat shot, or how to hit solid chips and pitches.
- Learning the relationship between path and clubface to shape shots.
- Learning about low point and how to create a proper divot.
- Having an intention for each round and staying committed to it.

When you commit to a process, you learn from your own experience, your awareness grows, and your skill develops.

Todd Graves knows a lot about process and developing skill; his Graves Golf Academy teaches a single-plane swing based on the swing of Moe Norman, regarded as the greatest ball-striker who ever lived.

Graves, a PGA of America professional, says "processes create consistency, and consistency makes outcomes measurable and predictable. When outcomes become measurable, adjustments can be made, and actions and decisions can be altered.

"Having a consistent process allows you to recognize variations and inconsistencies," he says.

The evidence is clear: if you try to take short cuts during the learning process and flit from tip to tip, you'll end up playing like garbage.

A Little Gratitude Takes You a Long Way

One of the best things you can do for your game and for your life is to develop a gratitude practice.

Given that our minds have a negative bias, practicing gratitude trains your mind to find perspective, dwell on moments of lightness, become more present, and cultivate a way of being that sees the golf course—and the world—as a place to savour, including the people you're with.

The following practice is similar to recording your three best experiences: At the end of the day, write down three things that you are grateful for from that day. It could be about your golf, your family, work, the weather, your mood, about an encounter with someone, a lovely sunset—whatever you feel grateful for.

The following are examples of gratitude entries:

- I'm thankful for my game with Trish today; I always enjoy my time with her.
- It was cool to birdie No. 4 after my bad start. I'm glad I didn't freak out with after my bogey-double start.

- I'm grateful that I trusted my pre-shot process down the stretch today. This kept me feeling calm and allowed me to swing freely.

- I'm grateful for my time in the car with my son today after his hockey practice. We had a great chat and really connected.

- This morning's sunrise was glorious. I took a picture of it and sent it to my sister.

- Thank goodness for Brad. The conversation was getting kind of feisty today, and he lightened everything up.

- I'm recovering well from my knee injury. I hope it continues to feel better.

Write as much or as little as you wish, and whatever you wish. There's no right way to do it. The easiest way to remind yourself to do this is to keep a notebook beside your bed. As with all these practices, the key is to commit.

I invite you to think about people you know who say "thank you" a lot. To me, they seem grounded, resilient, accepting, and less prone to freaking out. The practice of gratitude also increases your skill of awareness. When you find yourself dwelling on how you hooked your opening drive into the next galaxy, you're more likely to catch yourself, shift, find your equilibrium again, and carry on.

You also become better at shaking off bad breaks, mistakes, and crappy performances, and learning from them. I love Anne Lamott's perspective: "You can look at what was revealed in the latest mess and say thanks for the revelation because it shows you some truth that you needed to know."[1]

When you're grateful for playing golf or enjoying a beautiful day with your partners, it's much easier to cope on the days your swing isn't in the slot. I'm not saying you should whistle a happy tune if you're hitting it sideways, but gratitude gives you a chance of making a better swing, and it might prevent you from decapitating or drowning a club.[2] Your clubs will thank you for being grateful.

Practicing gratitude and writing about it also increases your ability to stay in the present moment. When you are grateful, you aren't judging. There are no "shoulds" or "coulds." You are accepting things as they are. You are practicing meta-awareness; you are aware in the moment that you are aware. And you are present.

Saying thank you to a person, to nature, God, the universe, or even a situation leads us to greater appreciation. We take so many things in this world for granted. It's rare that we think about how blessed we are to play golf—whether it's on a nine-hole cottage course with mats for tee decks or a posh country club—and by extension that we have the financial means, health, freedom, and the ability to enjoy all that a golf course has to offer.

I'm a big proponent of saying thanks to the golf course personnel for providing me with an opportunity to play golf. If I run into the course maintenance crew and superintendent, I also try to say thanks. I think that their skill in creating the conditions that we

---

[1] Anne Lamott. Help, Thanks, Wow: Three Essential Prayers. Riverhead Books. Page 49)

[2] In his "pre-enlightenment days," Howard said he was always two swings from a complete meltdown. Golf clubs that used to belong to him adorn the bottom of each pond at his former club, The National Golf Club of Canada, in Toronto.

enjoy in golf is close to otherworldly. My paltry excuse for a back-yard lawn usually looks like hell; they keep 250 acres looking like heaven. (I presume, of course, that heaven is all bentgrass.)

I also thank the golf course. Yes, the golf course.

About 15 years ago, I began to thank my golf course during my last round of the year. It's become a ritual to thank the course for the season it has provided me. Sure, that's weird but stay with me.

During my last round of the year, I like to play solo if possible because it allows me to have an uninterrupted experience in silence except for the wind, the birds, and the sound of my feet on the turf; the stillness feels sacred.

As I walk, my intention is to keenly observe and notice the nuances and beauty of the course, trees, bunkers, hills, and valleys. Everything around me. "Senses working overtime," as the XTC song goes.

I almost always notice things that I never saw before such as an interesting tree or roll in a fairway, and I've been playing my course for more than 20 years. It's like a walking meditation.

As I walk off the green of every hole, I try to remember to say thank you for the season. I'm often reminded of my great shots and atrocious ones, my good and bad decisions, or a funny line that a buddy said or an intriguing conversation. It's like I'm running my emotional highlight reel. It reminds me of key insights, breakthrough feelings, and important lessons I learned during the season.

I grant you that it's weird to say goodbye and thank you to a golf course, but it usually takes something radical to make a difference in our auto-pilot lives. When we're grateful, we experience and appreciate what's real and important.

That doesn't seem so weird, eh?

We spend most of our time in our heads, narrating our game, searching for swing fixes, making judgments about ourselves and others, caught in our stories, thinking, thinking, thinking. When we're locked in the dark space inside our craniums, we also don't see what the course is challenging us to consider. When we're lost in our stories or focused on mechanics, we often don't notice key elements that would greatly affect a shot, such as a crosswind or the slope of a green.

Appreciating the quirks of a golf course and adapting to them is one of the subtle charms of golf and a key to scoring. You may pure a shot, but if your assessment was off because you didn't notice something, your shot will usually be unsatisfactory.

When you practice gratitude, and soak in a course as something to behold and experience, you feel and think better. Gratitude makes you a better golfer and person.

Things to do to get unstuck

- Keep your gratitude journal beside your bed (this will remind you to write in it nightly).
- Write out three things that you're grateful for from the day; if you want to write more, go for it.
- Review a bunch from time to time, especially when you need a pick-me-up.
- Note how this practice blends into your golf and your day.

The gift of gratitude

One of the many cool things about doing the *Swing Thoughts* podcast for over nine years and more than 250 episodes with Howard Glassman is that we get to talk to many fascinating people, including folks from the world of golf, psychology, academia, and even stand-up comedy.

We call folks who have been frequent guests "Friend of Show" or FOS, such as Dick Zokol, Paul Dewland, Ed Coughlan, the late George McNamara, Charles Fitzsimmons, and Robert Damron. These folks are fascinating as experts, but they're also fun to talk to. Some have become friends.

This includes Karl Morris, a performance coach based in Britain. Karl has earned Hall of Fame status as an FOS. He's worked with Darren Clarke, Graeme McDowell, Lee Westwood and many more, and has many great stories and insights to share.

Sean Foley turned me on to Karl about 25 years ago. Since then, I've studied Karl's books, CDs, gone through some of his trainings, and become a big fan of his *Mind Caddie* podcast. He's become a mentor and even coached me.

During episode #184, Karl shared a story that was a little different; this time he was at the centre of the story. Karl related that a routine medical examination in early 2021 indicated some heart trouble. After some tests, it turned out that two heart arteries were 96 to 98 per cent blocked.

"It was a huge shock," he said. At the time, Karl said he was feeling great, doing high-intensity cardio and vigorous weight training. "I never felt fitter in my life." He felt OK because tributaries had grown in his heart to make up for the blockages. "These kept me alive."

In September of that year, he underwent quadruple bypass surgery. Unfortunately, he had to deal with numerous subsequent complications that made it unsafe for him to work out, hike, or walk while he plays golf. "It's been tough," he said. "I've played a few par-fives into the wind the last few weeks."

While the experience was scary, it brought him some perspective that has significantly influenced his approach to golf and life. "It reinforced to me the idea of gratitude and appreciation," he said. "It can sound trite when you're buzzing through life and you think there's always another round to play, then all of a sudden life goes, 'Uh oh, I have a message for you: Don't assume you have another season to play.'

"'What if you could be grateful for what you have today?'"

Gratitude is bandied about a lot in self-help and mindfulness circles, but some folks don't take it seriously. It's too nice. Kind of like having a cup of herbal tea and a bath when you can't sleep. Lest you think this interlude is just gooey-McMindfulness treacle, consider this: Gratitude is a recipe for playing great golf.

Karl said: "If you're going to play well, you have to be present to the puzzle that the golf course is presenting to you right now in this moment. That simple concept is very hard to do when you're constantly thinking, 'I'll be happy when I win a major, get enough money.'

"The more I look at it, gratitude is a foundational position for peak performance; the best expression you have on a given day."

Thanks Karl.

Transform Your Game by Changing Your Stories

By now, it's obvious that I'm biased that writing is a powerful tool that can assist golfers in transforming their self-defeating behaviours and moving forward. In this chapter, I'm referring to a specific form of writing called "story editing."

But it's not just personal preference. There's plenty of evidence from the world of social psychology that writing is a transformative tool. The work of James W. Pennebaker and Timothy D. Wilson, among other academics, corroborates it.

"Story editing tries to change people's personal interpretations of themselves … in ways that lead to more desirable behaviours," Wilson writes in *Redirect*. "People are directed to replace self-defeating thinking patterns." Wilson says you end up with a more desirable way of viewing yourself that leads to sustained change.[1]

---

[1] Timothy D. Wilson. *Redirect: The Surprising New Science of Psychological Change.* Little Brown. Pages 18-19.

A professor emeritus at the University of Texas, Pennebaker's work on "expressive writing" has shown that writing about our difficulties allows us to find solutions, perspective, and even strategies to overcome them. Pennebaker's book *Opening Up: The Healing Power of Expressing Emotions* contains several techniques used by coaches and therapists to assist players and clients to resolve difficult situations and issues. Wilson's book *Redirect* also has a number of excellent exercises.

I believe golfers can also use expressive writing to work through bad memories, disappointments, distressing events, and upsetting experiences that we all go through. It's especially helpful for events that you continue to think about and relive, whether they happened during your last round or 40 years ago. When we have a disturbing and emotional experience, we usually carry it forward. We also interpret these experiences, label them, and take messages from them that we use to define ourselves and our abilities.

For example, a golfer might determine that he "choked" down the stretch of a tournament. Or a player might miss several short putts to lose a match and determine she's "terrible" from short range. Or a player feels he is doomed to "always hitting it in the water on 12."

As per our section on memory, long after an incident, when we encounter situations that are like the original event, we're often triggered.[2] It's like we relive the same emotions, physical

---

[2] Like the word "trauma," some medical professionals say "trigger" is often misused, such as when someone refers to something they dislike, or causes a negative or unpleasant emotion. The more accurate use of trigger is when something can provoke unpleasant memories, cause you

sensations and even thinking. This occurs because the brain encodes incidents in which we experience high emotion so that we can recall them quickly. Again, it's the brain's way of trying to protect us from pain.

Depending on the severity of the experience, we can have a reaction known as fight, flight or freeze. This happens when the brain perceives a threat. We go on high alert, provoking a reaction in our body that prepares us to fight, flee, or freeze. You've experienced this, for example, if you've heard a loud noise, and suddenly stop, tense up and look around in fear.

When we're highly triggered, our body reacts: the stress hormone cortisol is released, our muscles tense, our heart rate accelerates, our breathing becomes shallow, and our blood moves toward our core to protect our organs (thus, we lose feeling in our hands). This puts us in a high arousal state ready for immediate action.

Golfers in this state cannot access their talent, experience, and skill, and they perform below their capabilities. In simple terms, their performance is impaired.

A woman told me during a workshop that during the final round of a club championship that she was leading, she faced a two-foot putt on the 17th hole. The head professional was watching from beside the green. As she was reading the putt, he said, "If you miss that, you can come to me for lessons." (Indeed, what a jerk!)

> to behave in ways you don't understand, or bring back feelings of fear. I believe it's appropriate in reference to golfers who have recurring struggles with certain shots or situations.

Under the circumstances, the remark rattled the woman and she began to think about what could happen if she missed. She did and went on to lose the championship. For the next two years, she struggled over every short putt she faced. I told her that she was re-experiencing feelings of fear and shock from the original incident. Unfortunately, I didn't have a chance to follow up with her.

I've coached several golfers who struggle with short putts, chip or driver yips, or they can't get out of bunkers. I'm often perceived as the coach of last resort. I deal a lot with golfers who are frustrated, overwhelmed, and hanging on to hope. Some say they're close to quitting golf. (Thankfully, most don't.) These players have tried everything: taking lessons, listening to friends, buying new clubs, incessantly watching YouTube, hypnosis, training devices, and self-medicating. These players are like addicts desperate for a fix![3]

All golf nerds suffer slumps, sometimes for a few rounds, but often for weeks or months, and sometimes an entire season can feel like an exercise in frustration, misery, and unrealized hopes. The most typical response is to flit from tip to trick to technique in a cycle of seeking, hoping, disappointment and yet more seeking.

As I've discussed, the cause of our problems—blow-up holes, nemesis shots, yips, slumps and more—is our thinking and

---

[3] Howard shared a story on our podcast about watching *Tin Cup* with his ex-wife. In the movie, the character played by Kevin Costner is suffering from a bout of the shanks just before the U.S. Open. When the movie gets to the scene where Costner is wearing a bunch of training devices in his trailer, Howard's ex-wife said, "You have all of those."

recurring behaviour patterns, rather than a lack of talent, bad habits, and bad luck. Unfortunately, we're often unaware of how past events influence our behaviours.

It's counter-intuitive to many golfers that their frustrations have origins similar to the stuff that you might tell a therapist. But you show up in golf the way you show up in the rest of your life, and you show up in your life the way you show up in golf. Addressing your thinking and behaviours, taking a look your beliefs and stories, and especially how you react to past events, allows you to see your behaviours in a much clearer light.

NEWSFLASH: MOST PEOPLE DON'T LIKE EXPLORING THEIR NEGATIVE THOUGHTS

It's natural to instinctively suppress your memories of troubling past events. Well, duh. You don't want dark and gloomy skies to cloud your golf or your mood. Thus, most people inhibit looking at their thoughts, feelings, and behaviours. This makes a problem worse. Again, what we resist persists.

According to Professor James Pennebaker, we do this intentionally. "Active inhibition means that people must consciously restrain, hold back, and in some way exert effort to not think, feel or behave."

Inhibition negatively affects our ability to think clearly about an event. "By not talking about an inhibited event, for example, we usually do not translate the event into language," he writes. This prevents us from understanding and "assimilating the event" and putting it in perspective. Consequently, we ruminate and "catastrophize" about significant experiences that we suppress.

Let's say you have a few rounds, for example, in which you chunk a few chips. So, you start to "work" on your chipping, borrowing a few swing thoughts from here and there. You apply them during your next round, and now you skull a few chips across the green. You determine that you're an "idiot" or worse. So you seek more information, and maybe a tip from your low-handicap buddy. But the chunks and skulls persist, and now your chipping stroke resembles a palsied stab. It gets so bad, you proclaim to the heavens, "I can't chip." You also hear your father's voice in your head: "Focus, you loser."

OK, that's a story, and you may think it's exaggerated, but it's a composite tale based on my experiences with clients. I consider the ones who come to me with the yips to be brave; indeed, they're often desperate, but it takes courage to talk about your struggles. Professor Brené Brown would call this being "vulnerable," a word that sends most men running for the hills. Unfortunately, this is most golfers, and they ain't talking.

Interestingly, Pennebaker also says "inhibition is physical work." Inhibition creates stress on the body that affects us during a round of golf, and over our life span. This explains, for example, why we tighten up on a hole that we've historically struggled with. Ask anyone with the first-tee jitters and you'll learn it's not their first rodeo.

Pennebaker says the opposite of inhibition is confrontation. While confrontation has a negative connotation, in this context we're talking about confronting your thinking and acknowledging your emotions as they relate to your golf and in other aspects of your life. "Confrontation reduces the effects of inhibition … (and) the biological stress of inhibition is immediately reduced. Over time, if individuals continue to confront and thereby resolve the trauma, there will be a lowering of the overall stress level on the body."

By confronting an experience—by talking or writing about it—you translate it into language. This helps you to understand, assimilate and recover from the event. Once that is done, you can better understand the experience, put it behind you and choose a course of action that will align with your mission or paradigm and commitments you've made to yourself.

In their work together, Sigmund Freud and colleague Josep Breuer said releasing pent-up thoughts and feelings provides a catharsis that "discharges psychic tension" in the same way that removing a lid from a pot of boiling water slows the boiling.[4]

PENNEBAKER'S PROCESS

Pick a topic or an event from your golf or life to write about. It's best to focus on an issue you are currently dealing with, especially if you find yourself dwelling on it. This is valuable for golfers who chronically struggle with a certain shot or situation and find themselves obsessed with solving it. It could be about—or connected to—an experience from a few weeks or months ago, or 25 years ago.

The best time to do this exercise is when you're fresh and unlikely to be disturbed. Set a timer for 15 minutes and begin free writing. Pennebaker advises that you explore the "objective experience"—what happened—as well as your feelings about it.

[4]James W. Pennebaker. *Opening Up: The Healing Power of Expressing Emotions*. The Guilford Press. Page 28.

"Really let go and write about your very deepest emotions," he writes. "What do you feel about it, and why you feel that way."

This exercise is especially valuable for things you're too embarrassed or afraid to tell someone else. In any case, what you're writing is for your eyes only. Pennebaker says that planning on showing your writing to someone may cause you to stay away from sensitive areas that would be valuable to explore. Make yourself the private audience.

Do the exercise for five days straight. (If you feel like writing more during the day or for longer than five days, go for it.) When you are finished, turn the pages over and let them be. Resist the temptation to immediately review them. You will find more value and gain greater insights when you read the pages much later when you've achieved some distance from the material.

After writing, you may feel strange, maybe sad, or angry, but these feelings usually recede after an hour or so.

Once they've completed the exercise in total, most people feel relief, happiness and contentment in the days and weeks to follow. Note that it's not a panacea that will make your negative feelings go away instantly, but you will have a better understanding of your thoughts and feelings and the objective situations you face on the golf course, or in the rest of your life. Writing provides perspective.[5]

---

[5] Here's a variation on the exercise that assists you in creating a new future that you can live into. Timothy D. Wilson suggests thinking about your life in the future and write for 20 minutes on four consecutive days, about "how everything has gone as well as it possibly could," and your dreams have come true.

This process will help you deal more effectively with your experiences and make better choices about the actions you take.

Let's be straight: feelings, beliefs, stories, and behaviours associated with the past don't "clear" or vanish because you have done some "work" on them. They've been a part of you for a long time, often for decades.

But by writing about them, meditating, talking about them, and even receiving some coaching, you will develop greater awareness that allows you to adapt and respond more skillfully. Even though old messages and feelings will still come up, the skill of awareness allows you to respond more quickly and appropriately based on your present reality. You are not tethered as tightly to your past. You can make choices that serve you as you are now.

Things to do to get unstuck

- When you are struggling, seeking to resolve, or to get some perspective on an experience, commit to write about it in your journal.
- Set a timer for 15 minutes and begin free writing.
- Do the exercise for five days straight.
- Reflect on the experience and whatever insights or perspective you have gained from the exercise.
- Flip the exercise as Wilson suggests in the footnote and write about your ideal future.

A model of inspiration for moving forward

If I hadn't run into Tim Casarin in the parking lot after my club championship, there's a good chance I could have done some violence to my clubs. Instead of hurling them into my car, I *placed* them. After changing my shoes, I stood by my car for a few seconds and stared at some maple trees swaying in the warm breeze. I shook my head as I thought about my encounter, and what a strange and wonderful thing it was.

Instead of heading home, I walked to the clubhouse and ordered a beer. I wandered over to the guys overlooking the 18th green. Of course, no one said anything about my four-putt. I remembered the classic golf axiom: no one cares about *your* round.

Looking out over the emerald green grass dappled with long shadows and at the epic blue sky, it occurred to me that, once again, I had succumbed to my self-pitying, raging, wailing ego. The dark, shadowy place where I've been going all my life. My stuck place.

Tim pulled me out of there. He gave me a gift with his presence, his example. He gave me a gift of grace.

I'm pretty sure that I thanked God at that moment for Tim Casarin, for the day, for being able to play golf at a course that I loved.

I was reminded that I'm not my golf scores, my stories, my reputation, my self-image, all my bullshit. That golf is better when I slightly don't care. When I treat it like a walk in the park as Moe Norman used to say.

When I make golf more than that, I flail around, enraged, disgusted, and mystified how I'm still doing this stupid, infantile nonsense. I know—I freaking know!—that my old ways create my own suffering and make me insufferable; these patterns have kept me stuck and caused me to look for love in many of the wrong places.

And that it's OK. As I said, I'm a golf nerd like you. As humans, we're going to screw up. My meltdowns, funks and foozles are reminders that I must stay awake and continue doing my work. Namely, do the practices that I've outlined in this book. Walk my talk.

As a golf nerd and a writer, I became fascinated by Tim Casarin. Namely, what inspires a man who was told by doctors that he'd likely never walk again without assistance to battle through immense pain and uncertainty to go back to work as a firefighter within a year?

Here's some of what I learned:

In May 2014, after coming out of his coma, Tim lay immobilized in the ICU of St. Michael's Hospital in Toronto—a thick Aspen cervical collar hugging his broken neck, a "fixator" drilled into his smashed pelvis with nine-inch nails like it was an aluminum girdle. Various pins, rods, and plates kept the majority of his 41 broken bones—including a busted right shoulder, fractured skull, and crushed right leg—"screwed together," he quipped.

As he stared at the ceiling for days, he worried if he'd ever get back to "normal," which certainly included playing golf.

During a routine conversation with his surgeon, Tim, through a mouthful of elastics and wires, mumbled: "When will I be able to play golf again?"

"That's not happening," the surgeon said, like he was giving directions to a lost motorist. "You'll be lucky to walk again without something to lean on."

Tim recalls the conversation. "I thought, 'Fuck you.' That's not where my mindset was. But I didn't worry about it. It was just 'next!'" He laughs at the memory: "I'm lying there half dead and I'm thinking, 'I have a round to play.'"

That Tim is playing golf again isn't the half of it.

In 2014, Tim was 46 and working as a full-time fire fighter in Mississauga, a suburb just west of Toronto. On April 23 at 4 a.m., Tim and his colleagues from Station 116 answered what appeared to be a routine call. Black smoke was leaking from a warehouse rooftop, and water was pouring out of some overhead doors. There were no flames. Whatever fire may have been burning appeared to be out.

Tim and two comrades went into the building but "couldn't see two inches in front of our faces" due to smoke. They headed for their truck to get some fans. That's the last thing he remembers.

Matt Attwell of Station 105 was helping a colleague back up an aerial truck when he saw Tim and two firefighters walk out of the building. Next, Matt heard what sounded like a bomb going off. The building exploded. The force of the blast pushed him forward.

"When I looked back, everyone was gone. I thought, 'Everyone is dead.' It looked like a war zone," Matt said.

"I thought, 'Today is the day I'm not going home.'"

He quickly figured out that the warehouse wall—about 20 feet high—fell on the trio. Matt and his colleagues raced toward the pile of rubble as flames rose high against the dark sky, dense smoke filled the air, and exploding propane and aerosol canisters hurtled around them like missiles.

They frantically pulled the shards of broken 50-pound cinderblocks off their buried friends. Matt said they found Tim lying face up, unconscious, barely breathing; his face was oddly smashed in, flattened, covered in blood. They dragged Tim and his two colleagues to ambulances. Some of Tim's fellow firefighters told me that they thought Tim would die.

(Matt and 10 others, including fire fighters and paramedics, were awarded Decorations for Bravery by the Governor General of Canada, along with other awards, for their role in rescuing Tim, Brad Hamilton, and Al Mills.)

Doctors at St. Michael's put Tim in a medically induced coma for eight days while they fought to stem massive internal bleeding. "It was a good two weeks before he was out of the woods," his son Jacob said.

Jacob, 16 at the time, said he glimpsed his father being wheeled into surgery. "That's when it really hit me. He didn't look human. It wasn't my dad. Just bones and skin and a lot of tubes."

Jacob and his sisters Hannah and Adelie stayed in a hotel

nearby and visited their father every day even though they couldn't communicate. Or so they thought. Adelie, who was in Grade 7 at the time, said that her father's brothers and sister spoke to him while he was in the coma, encouraging him to fight and live. Glumly, they said that he didn't respond.

But Adelie said she and her siblings had a different experience when they entered Tim's room in ICU: "The minute he heard our voices, his eyes started to blink, and his toes started to move. The nurses said it was first time he moved, and it was obvious he knew it was us."

Remarkably, within three weeks, with the aid of nurses and a walker, Tim could hop up to 20 times on his left leg, largely to prevent blood clots. "I never felt so exhausted," he said. "I was sweating."

After five weeks, Tim was wheeled into West Park Healthcare Centre in Toronto on a stretcher to begin his rehabilitation. Along with other complications, his right foot jutted awkwardly to the right as he stepped. Tim was distraught when he looked in the mirror.

"I was afraid of what I was," he said. "The speed of my recovery was way behind my motivation and where I wanted to be." By June, he graduated from a wheelchair to a walker to an aluminum cane.

Although Tim thought his recovery was slow, his family, friends, nurses, and doctors were amazed by the pace of his progress. Jacob remembers how his father relentlessly kept moving forward.

"At one point, he was told he'd never walk again. And then later they said that he would be able to stand but he wouldn't be able to do anything. Then he'd prove them wrong," said Jacob, now 27.

"Every nurse and doctor said, 'This guy is special.' The strongest guy they ever met. Any normal person would have given up, quit, or die. Not him. His strength was his will to live, get better and not accept he couldn't walk or play golf."

In August, at a family outdoor event, he was teetering along when someone said, "Watch the old man with the cane."

"I smashed the cane in half over a big rock—but not in anger," Tim said. "I always thought that I was the luckiest guy alive. I thought, 'I don't need this crutch.'"

On August 24, while in London, Tim thought it was time. "Just take one swing," he said. They drove to West Haven Golf Club. "I was terrified. I thought, 'Maybe I can't do this.' But I thought that I had to face these fears."

He nervously set up over the ball and swung. He stayed upright and connected. "It was really emotional. It was four months after the surgeon said I wouldn't walk again. I thought, 'OK, we got this.' When something positive happened, it motivated me to keep going."

In the fall of 2014, he played golf for the first time—riding in a cart—for 18 holes. "It was awesome. I was getting normalcy back."

Remarkably, in April 2015, he returned to work a year after the accident, earning him the name "Miracle Man" from his colleagues. His story was eagerly told in local and national media. Seven months later, he needed more surgery—his 27th—on his right leg to relieve pain and to remove some screws and pins.

Tim returned to active duty again in late 2016 and has since retired. He played more golf, although having lost flexibility in his hips and shoulders and strength in his legs, he devised a new swing.

Despite his incredible recovery, Tim doesn't see himself as a hero. He was just inspired. "I always feel like I got a second chance. When I look back at my recovery, that's one of the things I'm proud of: it was just day to day. That's why I worked my butt off—to see my kids and get back to whatever normal is."

Just before the 2023 season, he joined Blue Springs, which is how Tim and I re-connected.

I asked him: "How many rounds did you play last year?"

Tim: "Only 123."

Wow.

That's a golf nerd.

Tim and I are working on a book about the warehouse accident and his inspiring story of recovery.

Getting Unstuck

f you've gotten this far, it's my guess that you are willing to consider that the practices in this book can help you transform the self-defeating behaviour patterns that have kept you stuck.

As a golf nerd, you're liable to dive in and do all of them, but I suggest you start with one. Once you feel you're in a groove and it's become a habit, then add another. And if you limit yourself to one or two, that's great. Trust the process. Your process.

I'm going to challenge you: Make a commitment. Fred Shoemaker's brilliant statement about transformation bears repeating: "The only freedom that I found in golf was through a structure, and the only freedom I've found was through a commitment."

Commitment is key. It's far too easy to dabble, make excuses when you're tired, busy, or you just don't feel like doing a practice. But the most valuable time to do any of these practices is when you feel crappy, and your head is swirling. There's gold in that crappy stuff in your head! Observing yourself allows you to see yourself more clearly in the moments that you *want* to transform.

It sucks that our bad days are our greatest teachers. You reveal far more about yourself on the days you blow up, puke on your FootJoys (metaphorically!), and shoot a million than on the days when your swing is smooth and your putts are dropping.

Indeed, let's be grateful for those rare moments of bliss, but it's when we face the ugly and least desirable parts of ourselves that we do the most important work. It's when we're in the states that we dread and wish would go away that we come face to face with our demons—the beliefs, stories and behaviours that run our lives.

We have a choice: we can deal with our demons, which leads us to transformation, or ignore them and distract ourselves. Unfortunately, most people do the latter. This is the choice you face. As a golf nerd, I believe that you have the tenacity, resilience, and courage to do the work, but you may not have known how. The practices in this book—all of which I've cobbled together from masters who came before me—are tools used by elite performers.

Working on your own can be tough. That's why it's valuable to have a coach or a buddy who can support you in your interior work. A coach holds up a mirror to you and provides perspective and guidance, but also holds your feet to the fire and keeps you accountable. A coach is not a cheerleader, but a practical guide and pillar who supports you to keep doing the hard work, especially when you don't want to.

You could also ask a trusted friend to hold you accountable. You might just find that over time you open up a bit more and discover how good it feels to share your deeper stuff, and how it takes relationships to a higher level.

Doing this kind of interior work is like working out: you get the greatest satisfaction when you push through your resistance. It's when you resist that you continue to flail, chase after rainbows and fixes.

But when you confront your beliefs, stories, and patterns of thinking and behaving, you reveal their toxicity, falsity, and deceitfulness. You diminish their power over you. Each time that you witness and deal with them, their hold decreases.

Your natural defence mechanism will be to resist looking at your negative thoughts and feelings; you will hide, repress, and deny them as if you were keeping them hidden under lock and key. These are the behaviours and habits that keep you stuck. To transform the patterns that have kept you underperforming requires expanding your awareness of those behaviours so you can address them and bring more of your strengths and grit to the task.

However, you *will* continue to have days when you feel bad, and you get caught in your stories and self-destructive behaviours. You're a human. We're messy. But having the awareness, for example, that "I'm in it" starts the process of working your way out.

Our society tells us that if we absorb knowledge and apply fixes to our supposed faults or shortcomings, we'll change, become great golfers, and finally be happy. Sorry. Doesn't happen. Nothing will change unless you integrate new ways of being and experiences into your life on a frequent, if not daily basis. Unless you integrate the practices, when you're under stress—such as a tournament, a highly anticipated round, or you're trying to finish a great round—you will fall back into the old behaviours; the same ones you've been falling back on since you were a kid.

The work is unrelenting. It never stops until your last breath. That's the challenge of being a human—of being a golf nerd.

It's tough sledding. If your desire is to become the golfer that you envision, your work includes developing your swing, taking care of your body, and learning how to use your mind more skillfully.

It also requires observing, making better choices, healing, nurturing your spirit and engaging in practices that increase your self-awareness. This is the hardest work you'll ever do. But it's also the most enriching and fulfilling work you will ever do—for your golf, and for your life, the people in your life, and your influence on the world.

Can golf really be a portal to that kind of transformation?

With all my heart, I believe it is.

SUGGESTED READING

Cameron, Julia. *The Artist's Way: A Spiritual Path to Higher Creativity*. Tarcher/Putman.

Coyle, Daniel. *The Talent Code: Greatness Isn't Born. It's Grown. Here's How*. Bantam.

Csikszentmihalyi, Mihaly. *Flow: The Psychology of Optimal Experience*. HarperPerrenial.

Enhanger, Kjell. *Quantum Golf: The Path to Golf Mastery*. Warner Books.

Gallwey, Timothy. *The Inner Game of Golf*. Random House.

Gallwey, Timothy. *The Inner Game of Tennis*. Random House.

Hebron, Michael. *Play Golf to Learn Golf*. Learning Golf, Inc.

Langer, Ellen. *Mindfulness*. Da Capo Press.

Merton, Thomas. *New Seeds of Contemplation*. New Directions Books.

Meyers, Susie. *Golf From Point A*. Point of View Productions, LLC.

Morris, Karl. *Attention: The Secret to YOU Playing Great Golf*. The London Press.

Morris, Karl and Nicol, Gary. *The Lost Art of Playing Golf*. Sports Publications Limited.

Murphy, Michael. *Golf in the Kingdom*. Penguin.

Nilsson, Pia, and Marriott, Lynn. *Every Shot Must Have a Purpose*. Gotham Books.

Nilsson, Pia, and Marriott, Lynn. *Be a Player: A Breakthrough Approach to Playing Better on the Golf Course.* Atria Books.

Pennebaker, James W. *Opening Up: The Healing Power of Expressing Emotions.* The Guilford Press.

Shoemaker, Fred, and Shoemaker, Peter. *Extraordinary Golf: The Art of the Possible.* Putman.

Shoemaker, Fred, and Hardy, Jo. *Extraordinary Putting: Transforming the Whole Game.* Penguin.

Vickers, Joan. *Perception, Cognition, and Decision Training.* Human Kinetics.

Wilson, Timothy D. *Redirect: The Surprising New Science of Psychological Change.* Little, Brown and Company.

Winkleman, Nick. *The Language of Coaching: The Art & Science of Teaching Movement.* Human Kinetics.

Zweig, Connie, and Abrams, Jeremiah, Editors. *Meeting the Shadow: The Hidden Power of the Dark Side of Human Nature.* Tarcher/Putman.

ACKNOWLEDGEMENTS

My greatest thanks go to my wife Sandy Halloran, who has both loved me and kicked my butt so that I would finally get this damn thing done.

I'm grateful to my sons Corey and Sean for being great guys and throwing my stuff back in my face when I didn't appear to be walking my talk.

I count my blessings for my mother Margaret and father Dennis, who introduced me to golf, nurtured my love for reading, and encouraged me to write.

Thanks to Lorne Rubenstein, John Gordon, and Bob Weeks—all giants of Canadian golf writing—for their support and influence. If not for them, I would never have taken the risk to write about this amazing game.

I could never say thank you enough to Howard Glassman—aka Humble Howard, a plus-handicap broadcaster and legend—for having the patience to persevere with me to co-host the *Swing Thoughts* podcast, which at this writing we've been delivering for nine seasons and shared more than 250 episodes. Thanks to Humble for reminding me that my superpower as a coach is that I delve into matters of the spirit and heart. And for helping me become about an 8-handicap broadcaster.

Thanks to marketing guru Len Kahn—and drumming kingpin—who said to stop talking about a book and write it, and to Kent Osborne who reminded me that, well, yeah, I'm a pretty good writer, and to finish and ship this book. Then start a new one the next day.

I've had a number of coaching mentors, but none more influential than Fred Shoemaker, who I've been fortunate to get to know along with his amazing partner Jo Hardy. I hope that I've sufficiently given credit where credit is due to Fred, who I'll argue will eventually become known as one of the greatest coaches in the history of the game.

In a similar way, I owe a tremendous thanks to Karl Morris, not only for sharing his insights on how to be great performer, but also for modeling how to communicate in a heartfelt and accessible way.

Thanks to Paul Dewland, a coach to many PGA and LPGA players and elite amateurs, who was instrumental as a coach, friend, and mentor in influencing me to jump into this coaching thing.

I'm extremely fortunate to be friends with Todd Graves, who has done more than anyone to both protect and increase awareness of the legend, Moe Norman. When I doubted in my abilities and depth of knowledge to coach golfers, Todd told me to get on my horse.

I've been the beneficiary of helpful private audiences with Dr. Ed Coughlan, a fine coach and with whom I proudly share Irish heritage.

Thanks to Sean Foley for his coaching those many years ago at Glen Abbey, and for being such an interesting, articulate, and authentic model.

Thanks to Tim Casarin for being an inspiration to thousands of people on how to persevere through unfathomable circumstances, and for being my angel in the parking lot.

This book—and indeed the work I do as a coach—would never have come to fruition without the influence of my brother Pat who led me to the ManKind Project, which allowed me to develop a greater awareness of our inner lives as men and to become a facilitator and coach. I'm indebted to men such as David Robinson, George Daranyi, Walter Sienko, Mike Barrington, Dave Tuscany and many more for their love and support.

Thanks to Kim Monteforte for her guidance in designing this book.

TIM O'CONNOR

This isn't who he is, but this is what Tim O'Connor does—and has done.

Tim is a writer, coach, speaker, workshop leader, podcaster, bass player, and golf nerd.

As an award-winning journalist, Tim was the national music writer for The Canadian Press news agency, freelance golf reporter for CBC-Radio, and freelance golf writer.

He has written four previous books including *The Feeling of Greatness: The Moe Norman Story; The Ladies: 1924-1999; Devil's Pulpit: The First Decade;* and he co-wrote *The Single Plane Golf Swing: Play Better Golf the Moe Norman Way* with Todd Graves.

Tim was inducted into the Golf Ontario Hall of Fame in 2020 as the winner of the Lorne Rubenstein Media Award.

He was a golf industry media consultant for 14 years before transitioning to coaching in 2014. He is former head coach of the men's and women's golf team at the University of Guelph.

He writes the *Up & Down* newsletter on the Substack platform. He is co-host of the *Swing Thoughts* podcast launched in 2015 with "Humble" Howard Glassman.

Along with mental game and life coaching, he coaches at The Golf House in Guelph and at Blue Springs in Acton, both in Ontario.

He plays bass in C.I.D., a vintage punk band based in Guelph, where he lives with his wife Sandy Halloran and their boxer Freddie. They have two sons, Corey and Sean.

To discuss coaching, workshops or speaking engagements, please send an email to

tim@oconnorgolf.ca

You can read Tim's newsletter on

toconnor.substack.com

His website and archived blogs are on

www.oconnorgolf.ca

TWITTER/X

x.com/timoconnorcoach

FACEBOOK

www.facebook.com/Tim57oConnor/

INSTAGRAM

www.instagram.com/oconnor7502/

9 781739 001995